0.0

2161   D0559999   0

Herbert Hoover

Titles in the United States Presidents *series:*

ABRAHAM LINCOLN
ISBN 0-89490-939-8

ANDREW JACKSON
ISBN 0-89490-831-6

ANDREW JOHNSON
ISBN 0-7660-1034-1

BILL CLINTON
ISBN 0-7660-1036-8

DWIGHT D. EISENHOWER
ISBN 0-89490-940-1

FRANKLIN D. ROOSEVELT
ISBN 0-7660-1038-4

GEORGE WASHINGTON
ISBN 0-89490-832-4

HARRY S. TRUMAN
ISBN 0-89490-833-2

HERBERT HOOVER
ISBN 0-7660-1035-X

JAMES MADISON
ISBN 0-89490-834-0

JAMES MONROE
ISBN 0-89490-941-X

JAMES K. POLK
ISBN 0-7660-1037-6

JIMMY CARTER
ISBN 0-89490-935-5

JOHN F. KENNEDY
ISBN 0-7660-1039-2

LYNDON B. JOHNSON
ISBN 0-89490-938-X

RICHARD M. NIXON
ISBN 0-89490-937-1

RONALD REAGAN
ISBN 0-89490-835-9

THEODORE ROOSEVELT
ISBN 0-89490-836-7

THOMAS JEFFERSON
ISBN 0-89490-837-5

WOODROW WILSON
ISBN 0-89490-936-3

United States Presidents

Herbert
Hoover

Series Consultant:
Don M. Coerver, professor of history
Texas Christian University, Fort Worth, Texas

David M. Holford

LEARNING RESOURCE CENTER
OLIVE C. MARTIN SCHOOL
24750 WEST DERING LANE
LAKE VILLA, IL 60046

Enslow Publishers, Inc.

40 Industrial Road	PO Box 38
Box 398	Aldershot
Berkeley Heights, NJ 07922	Hants GU12 6BP
USA	UK

http://www.enslow.com

For Alex, who shares his father's love of history.

Copyright © 1999 by David M. Holford

All rights reserved.

No part of this book may be reproduced by any means
without the written permission of the publisher.

Library of Congress Cataloging-in-Publication Data

Holford, David M.
  Herbert Hoover / David M. Holford.
    p. cm. — (United States presidents)
    Includes bibliographical references (p. 116) and index.
    Summary: A biography of Herbert Hoover, thirty-first president of
  the United States, describing his career as mining engineer,
  businessman, and president during the Great Depression.
    ISBN 0-7660-1035-X
    1. Hoover, Herbert, 1874–1964—Juvenile literature. 2. Presidents—
  United States—Biography—Juvenile literature. [1. Hoover, Herbert,
  1874–1964. 2. Presidents.] I. Title. II. Series.
  E803.H675   1999
  973.91'6'092—dc21
  [B]   98-11688
                                                      CIP
                                                       AC

Printed in the United States of America

10 9 8 7 6 5 4 3 2

To Our Readers:
All Internet addresses in this book were active and appropriate when
we went to press. Any comments or suggestions can be sent by e-mail to
Comments@enslow.com or to the address on the back cover.

Illustration Credits: AP/Wide World Photos, pp. 24, 83; Boys and
Girls Clubs of America Archives, p. 109; Esther and Violet Witmer, p. 18;
Herbert Hoover Presidential Library, pp. 12, 13, 16, 31, 33, 39, 42, 46, 52,
55, 60, 64, 86, 87, 94, 101, 102; Hoover Institution Archives, p. 6; Robert
M. Friedman, p. 113; UPI/CORBIS-BETTMAN, p. 57.

Source Document Credits: *Albany Times Union*, p. 90; Harry S.
Truman Library, p. 105; Herbert Hoover Presidential Library, pp. 10, 41,
89; *Public Papers of the Presidents of the United States: Herbert Hoover*, vol.
1 (1929), Washington: Government Printing Office, 1974, p. 66; Scripps-
Howard, p. 76; *West Branch Times*, p. 20.

Cover Illustration: Hoover Presidential Library Association.

Contents

1   The Bonus Army..............................   7

2   The Orphan from Iowa......................   15

3   Stanford Pioneer   27

4   The Globetrotter..............................   36

5   Food Regulator of the World   48

6   The Wonder Boy..............................   59

7   Good Times and Bad   68

8   Blame It on Hoover   79

9   The Wilderness Years and After........   93

10   Legacy 106

    Chronology...................................114

    Chapter Notes 116

    Further Reading 124

    Places to Visit and
    Internet Addresses 125

    Index 127

Former president Hoover poses in front of Hoover Tower on the campus of Stanford University.

1

THE BONUS ARMY

From the White House window President Herbert Hoover watched the flames climbing in the dark summer sky. He realized at once what was on fire. The knowledge horrified and sickened him. Ignoring Hoover's orders, General Douglas MacArthur had sent the United States Army into action against American citizens who were camped in the capital. Now their shacks and meager possessions were burning.

The president thought about the public outcry that was sure to follow. He weighed his alternatives. This year, 1932, was an election year. He already faced a tough reelection fight. Should he let people know that MacArthur had ignored his order not to launch the attack? Or should he take the blame for the incident himself? Hoover decided on the second course of action. It was a bad choice.[1]

The nation was in a deep depression in 1932. An economic depression is a severe cutback in business activity. It is accompanied by high unemployment, falling prices and wages, and sometimes by rioting. The depression that began while Hoover was president lasted until about 1940. It is called the Great Depression because its effects were felt worldwide, making it the worst economic downturn in modern history. Millions of people did not have enough to eat. In the United States, many people saw their savings disappear. They lost all hope for the future.

One group of Americans, however, had something of monetary value. Veterans, or former soldiers, who had fought in World War I each had a certificate from the United States government worth one thousand dollars. Congress had issued these bonus certificates to the veterans in 1924, to be payable in 1945.

By 1932, however, the Depression was near its lowest point. More than one out of every four workers was unemployed. Many were veterans who did not want to wait thirteen more years for the money that was promised them. They needed it immediately. Other Americans, including many members of Congress, opposed the veterans' demand. They were supported by President Herbert Hoover. He thought the government could not afford to make these payments.[2]

In May 1932, a group of veterans from Oregon headed to Washington, D.C. They planned to ask Congress to pay the bonus early. As they moved eastward, more veterans joined them. By the time the group arrived in Washington, it had grown to about one thousand members.

The nation's press reported the story of the cross-country trek. They nicknamed the ragtag band the "Bonus Army." The newspaper reports convinced other veterans to head for Washington. Throughout the month of May, they streamed into the city, many with their wives and children. By early June about twenty thousand people had assembled. Many of them set up camp in Anacostia Park in the eastern part of the capital.

Even if he had not been involved in a campaign for reelection, Hoover would have treated the Bonus Army with kindness. Although he opposed their cause, he believed most of the soldiers to be good Americans. He provided them with food, medical supplies, blankets, tents, and other Army equipment. However, he would not meet with their leaders.

Each day, veterans filled the halls of Congress, trying to see their senators and congressmen. They held huge marches down Pennsylvania Avenue. They demonstrated at the Capitol and at the White House. In order to survive, some begged door-to-door in neighborhoods. Others loitered downtown, seeking handouts on the streets. Government officials grew worried about their obtrusive presence.

On June 17, Congress defeated a bill to pay the bonus early. When the government offered them free train tickets to go home, several thousand veterans refused to leave. "We'll stay here until 1945 if necessary," one leader vowed.[3] However, many of them left their muddy camp in Anacostia Park. They took over

SOURCE DOCUMENT

Oregon Contingent, B.E.F.

8th and I Street. S.E.

Washington D.C. July 25th, 19

PETITION.

To Whom It May Concern at the White House,   *file*

Dear Sirs:-

The bearers of this petition most respectfully request a brief interview, either with President Hoover, or some fully qualified person acting in his behalf, for the purpose of presenting a practical, legal and constitutional, plan for a prompt settlement of the trouble and unrest now prevailing in the District of Columbia arising out of the recent decision of Congress to refuse immediate payment of the veteran's adjusted compensation certificates.

The proposal we have to present can be fully explained in less than fifteen minutes.

Respectfully Submitted:

E.J. Mun ce.
Commander. 1st Regiment.

Albert W oot
Chief of Staff. 1st Regiment.

Samuel Bottomby
Financial Advisor. 1st Regiment
137 Wickliffe St.
Newark, New Jersey

Bonus Army veterans from Oregon presented the White House with this request for a meeting with the president. Advised that the Bonus Army leaders were Communists and troublemakers, Hoover refused their request.

unused government offices and other abandoned buildings in downtown Washington.

As June passed into July, Congress adjourned. The demonstrations continued, however. Hoover's advisers convinced him that most of the decent veterans had gone home. Those who remained, they said, were largely criminals and other troublemakers.[4] The president ordered these stragglers to vacate government property. As tensions increased, the White House gates were closed and chained.

Finally, on July 28, police began to clear veterans from some of the empty buildings they had occupied. A brief riot broke out when the veterans resisted. City officials turned to the president for help. Reluctantly, Hoover called for the Army. "There is no group, no matter what its origins, that can be allowed to violate the laws of this city or to intimidate [threaten] the government," he explained.[5]

About eight hundred troops under the command of General Douglas MacArthur assembled behind the White House and moved down Pennsylvania Avenue toward the Capitol. Rush hour was under way. Homeward-bound workers were shocked to see troops and tanks on the streets of their capital.

Hoover had told MacArthur to push the Bonus Army out of the downtown area and back to its camp. "Use all humanity consistent with the due execution of this order," the president insisted.[6] However, MacArthur had his own ideas about what needed to be done. He ordered the troops forward. Journalist Frederick Lewis Allen described what happened next:

Members of the Bonus Army camp out on the Capitol lawn in July 1932, after a long day of demonstrations.

Suddenly there was chaos: cavalrymen were riding into the crowd, infantrymen were throwing tear-gas bombs, women and children were being trampled and were choking from the gas; a crowd of three thousand or more spectators who had gathered in a vacant lot . . . were being pursued by the cavalry and were running wildly . . . screaming as they stumbled and fell. The troops moved slowly on, scattering veterans and homegoing government clerks alike.[7]

As the veterans retreated to Anacostia Park, Hoover told MacArthur not to pursue them. However, the general defied the president again. He ordered his troops into the veterans' camp and burned it. Flames shot two hundred feet into the air. The veterans saved what they could of their few possessions and fled into the night. MacArthur's aide, Major Dwight D. Eisenhower, described it as "a pitiful scene."[8]

Smoke fills the air as soldiers patrol a burned-out camp following the attack on the Bonus Army on July 28, 1932.

MacArthur later defended his actions to reporters. "That mob down there was a bad-looking mob," he explained.[9] At the White House, the president issued a similar statement: "A challenge to the authority of the United States government has been met, swiftly and firmly. . . . Government cannot be coerced [forced] by mob rule."[10]

Later, in private, Hoover severely criticized MacArthur for his actions.[11] But Hoover's public response had been a mistake. Across the nation, the press condemned the president for the attack. When Democratic presidential candidate Franklin D. Roosevelt heard about the incident, he said, "This will elect me."[12] He was right. The Bonus Army had disappeared. With it went Hoover's remaining chances for reelection.

For years before he was elected, Herbert Hoover was considered better qualified to be president than any other American. His election in 1928 was one of the greatest landslides in American political history. But just four years later, Hoover was the most hated person in the land. For an entire generation of Americans, the name Hoover was forever tied to inhumanity, failure, and disgrace.

Hoover carried the blame for the Great Depression from his defeat in 1932 until his death more than thirty years later. Only in recent times have people begun to view him in a more favorable light. The astonishing rise and rapid fall of the man once called the "Wonder Boy" and his long effort to rebuild his reputation make one of the greatest stories in the history of American politics.

2

THE ORPHAN FROM IOWA

From all appearances, Jesse Hoover and Hulda Minthorn made an unlikely couple. Jesse was tall and bearded, friendly and cheerful. He was known throughout the small, east Iowa town of about three hundred fifty people for his sense of humor. He worked with his hands. Hulda was shy, quiet, and very serious. A teacher, she was well educated for a woman of the 1870s.

Yet Jesse and Hulda shared a common background. Both were children of pioneers. Each was determined to succeed. In 1854, eight-year-old Jesse and his family had come by covered wagon from Ohio. They settled to farm near the new town of West Branch, Iowa. Hulda arrived from Canada with her family in 1859. She was eleven. The Minthorns also settled on a farm just outside of town.

Like almost everyone else in West Branch, the Hoovers and the Minthorns were Quakers. No one knows for sure where Jesse first noticed Hulda. It might have been in the school they both attended. Maybe it was at the silent worship services that Quakers call "meeting." However, Jesse was impressed by Hulda's deep faith.[1]

In March 1870, Jesse and Hulda married. They purchased the lot next to the blacksmith shop he had opened in town. There Jesse and his father built a small, three-room cottage for the new couple. Their first child, Theodore or "Tad," was born in 1871. A few years later a second son arrived. Hulda's eldest sister, Ann, suggested they name the boy Herbert.

Herbert Hoover's parents, Hulda and Jesse, had been married for about nine years in 1879, when these photos were taken.

Herbert Clark Hoover was born on August 10, 1874. The birth occurred at just about midnight. In the excitement no one bothered to note the exact time. Bertie, as he was called, began life as a cheerful baby. However, he soon was plagued by periods of harsh coughing and difficult breathing. Today, doctors would probably diagnose Bertie's problem as asthma, but that condition was not known in the 1800s.

One day, when Bertie was about two, he had a very bad attack. Hulda's brother, John Minthorn, was the local doctor, but he was not at home. Bertie's panicked parents summoned other relatives. Nothing anyone did was able to stop his gasping for breath.

Suddenly Bertie went limp! Believing the boy was dead, his family laid him on a table and covered him with a sheet. Then someone noticed a faint movement beneath the sheet. At that moment, Dr. Minthorn rushed in. He had just returned from visiting a patient outside of town. The doctor revived the toddler. Grandmother Minthorn announced to the assembled relatives: "God has a great work for that boy to do; that is why he was brought back to life."[2]

Religion was a central part of life in the Hoover household. Card playing, dancing, and alcohol were forbidden. Hulda held weekly prayer gatherings in their home. She required Jesse and the children to attend "meeting" at the church twice a week. Young Bertie sat quietly through these long sessions of silent prayer and reflection. Hoover later remembered that this experience was "strong training in patience."[3]

When Bertie was about four years old, his father

Herbert Hoover was born in this small cottage in West Branch, Iowa, on August 10, 1874.

started a new business making farm equipment. As the business prospered, Jesse sold the cottage and black-smith shop.

The family had grown again with the birth of a daughter, Mary, in 1876. In 1879, the Hoovers moved to a larger house a few blocks away. Later that year, Hulda enrolled her younger son in the town's public school. The boy proved to be only an average student. However, he had a great curiosity.

One day Bertie wondered what would happen if he tossed a burning stick into a kettle of tar that his father used to coat barbed wire to prevent rust. Flames shot from the kettle, and a huge column of smoke billowed across the town. The little boy fled in terror. Only the townspeople's help kept his father's business from being destroyed by fire. Another experiment, carving wood with a knife, nearly cost Bertie a finger.

When the youngster was not conducting "experiments" or trying to reach China by digging a hole in the front yard, he awaited other adventures. West Branch had recently been on the western frontier. There were still woods to explore and streams to dam for swimming. Bertie developed a love of fishing that lasted the rest of his life. Because of the Quakers' belief in nonviolence, the brothers were not allowed to handle guns. So American Indian boys from a nearby government school taught them to hunt with bows and arrows.

Shortly after Bertie's sixth birthday, his carefree life came to an end. In December 1880, Jesse fell ill. Tad and Bertie were sent to visit Uncle Benjah Hoover while their father recovered. A few days later, word arrived to return the boys home. Jesse had died at the age of thirty-four.

The tragedy brought major changes. Uncle Benjah took over the business, and Hulda took in sewing to support her three children. Later, for additional income, she rented out a room of the house.

Relatives helped the family, too. The husband of Hulda's sister Agnes had been put in charge of an American Indian reservation in what is now part of Oklahoma. To ease the burdens on her sister, Agnes took young Bertie home to live with her family for a while. For several months, he attended the school on the reservation and played with Osage Indian boys. During this time his lifelong love of nature and the outdoors became even stronger.[4]

Her husband's death only strengthened Hulda's already deep religious faith. Increasingly, she felt a call to preach. In the spring of 1883, Mrs. Hoover became a minister in the Society of Friends. This is what Quakers call their Church. She soon became known in Quaker communities throughout Iowa and beyond. The demand for Hulda's preaching sometimes kept her away from home for two to three weeks at a time. During these periods the children stayed with friends and relatives in West Branch.

SOURCE DOCUMENT

sadly crooning, "Dear Mother, I've come home to Die."

—Much smoke and a big scare Saturday afternoon a cauldron of tar which J. C. Hoover was heating for a coating for fence wire took fire and immediately great clouds of fire and smoke were sent up, causing much excitement among our people. Everybody with buckets in hand, rushed pell mell for the scene of the conflagration which was midway between Hoover's agricultural house and Rummels & White's meat market. A copious application of water soon quieted the fire which caused no damage other than the destruction of the cauldron of tar.

—One of the happiest events of Christmas day, was the reunion of the

This report appeared in the West Branch Local Record *on New Year's Day, 1880. It describes the fire Bertie accidentally set in his father's factory that nearly burned down the business.*

In February 1884, tragedy again struck the Hoover household. While conducting a revival meeting, Hulda became ill with typhoid fever. On her way home, she also developed pneumonia. Three days later, Hulda was dead. She was only thirty-five years old. At the age of nine, Bertie Hoover was an orphan.

None of Hulda's relatives were still in the area. With many other settlers, they had left West Branch in 1879, after a religious disagreement developed among local Quakers. Following Hulda's wishes, seven-year-old Mary went to stay with Grandmother Minthorn, who was now living in western Iowa. Thirteen-year-old Tad was sent to Jesse's brother, Davis Hoover, whose home was in the central part of the state.

Mollie Brown, Bertie's teacher, offered to take Bertie in. But because she was not married, the family judged her unsuitable to raise a child. Instead, the boy went to live with Uncle Allen, another of Jesse's brothers, on a farm near West Branch. In this manner, Hulda's three children were scattered across the state. The two thousand dollars she had saved for their education was turned over to a legal guardian, to be used to pay for their upbringing.

Herbert Hoover considered the year and a half when he lived on his uncle's farm a pleasant interlude. Yet, without even realizing it, he never lost the sense of being an outsider. Later, those who did not really know him judged Hoover to be distant, reserved, and even unfeeling. The time on Uncle Allen's farm seems to have been when these traits started to develop. He may have begun to put a protective "shell" around his true feelings to help hide his loneliness.[5]

In the fall of 1885, a letter arrived from John Minthorn, who had saved Bertie's life when he was two. Dr. Minthorn was now living in Newberg, Oregon, where he and his wife had started a Quaker school. Uncle John and Aunt Laura had recently lost their only son, and they asked Bertie to come live with them.

Newberg was even smaller than West Branch. However, the relatives believed the boy could get a better education there. So on November 10, 1885, with twenty cents in his pocket and carrying a huge basket of food prepared by his aunt, Bertie boarded a train for Oregon. There he would spend the rest of his youth.

When he arrived in Newberg, Hoover was enrolled at the Friends Pacific Academy. Although the eleven year old was the smallest student at the school, his childish nickname had already given way to the more adult-sounding "Bert."

Again, Bert earned only average grades—except in mathematics, in which he excelled. Now, because the Minthorns did not share their Iowa relatives' objections to literature, he was able to read widely both at school and in his uncle's library.

John Minthorn was brilliant and talented, but he was also stern and demanding. He believed that Bert's parents had not taught him discipline or the value of hard work.[6] Minthorn required Bert to milk the cow nightly, split wood for the fireplace, feed and water the horses twice a day, and hitch up the team whenever the doctor needed to travel by buggy. "As time went on I was introduced to harder tasks," Hoover reported later.[7]

On the Sabbath, the boy was required to go to meeting and Sunday school, attend meetings of a Quaker youth group, and spend the rest of the day in Bible study. Uncle John also expected Bert to go with him on long trips into the countryside to visit medical patients. On these trips, Bert learned about physiology, or the parts and structure of living things.

Uncle John meant well and was trying to teach Bert responsibility. However, the stubborn teenager often complained to other relatives about his treatment, which he believed was too harsh. Minthorn later recalled, "He [Bert] always seemed to me to resent ever being told to do anything."[8]

Despite all his duties, Bert was still able to find time to play baseball, explore the outdoors, and pursue his beloved fishing. Yet people who knew Hoover during this period remembered him as a very serious young man.[9] His loneliness lessened for a short time when, in September 1887, brother Tad arrived to attend the academy. Like Bert, Tad frequently clashed with his strict uncle.[10]

In the summer of 1888, John Minthorn resigned as head of the academy. The family took Bert to Salem, Oregon, a bustling city of eight thousand people. There Minthorn entered the real estate business. The move brought more changes for Bert. Grandmother Minthorn and sister Mary soon moved from Iowa to Salem. But once again he was separated from Tad, who remained in school at Newberg. In addition, Bert had to work as

The Hoover children had been orphans for four years when this picture was taken in 1888. Bert, on the right, was about fourteen years old.

an office boy in his uncle's new business. At age fifteen, his education appeared to be at an end.

Over the next two years, Bert threw himself into Minthorn's business. Another of Minthorn's employees described Bert's work during this time:

> Herbert Hoover was the quietest, the most efficient, and the most industrious boy I ever knew in an office. He even wore quiet shoes and you never knew he was around until you wanted something, and then he was right at your elbow. He knew everything about the office and the rest of us never tried to keep track of things. It was easier and quicker just to ask Bert about it.[11]

For a while, Bert considered making a career of real estate. When a business school opened in Salem, Bert enrolled in night classes. "My boyhood ambition," Hoover later recalled, "was to be able to earn my own living, without the help of anybody, anywhere."[12]

During this period Bert got to know two people who would change his life. One was an engineer who often stopped by the real estate office. The other was a woman named Jane Gray, whose goal was to help boys who had quit school and gone to work. She introduced the young office boy to the great works of literature.

Because of their influence, Bert decided that he wanted to go to college and study engineering.[13] But where would an orphan who had hardly any money get a college education? His relatives could help him get a scholarship at Earlham College, a Quaker school in Indiana. However, it did not offer engineering courses. Instead, Bert decided to seek admission to Stanford University, a new college that was opening in northern California. Here students could attend classes for free.

"A general education is the birthright of every man and woman in America," claimed Leland Stanford, the college's founder.[14] In addition, because they needed students, college officials were willing to overlook the fact that Bert had not finished high school. All he had to do was pass the university's entrance examination.

The entrance exam showed Bert to be almost completely unprepared to attend college. He failed in every subject but mathematics. However, Professor John Swain, who supervised the test, saw something special in this quiet, serious Quaker boy. He suggested that Bert come to the university three months early, hire a tutor, and prepare to take the test again.[15]

So in June 1891, Bert Hoover, not yet seventeen years old, headed for California. He took one hundred sixty dollars that he had saved while working for his uncle. Minthorn gave him an additional fifty dollars and offered the boy his blessings. Bert would face the hardest summer of his young life if he hoped to attend college in the fall.

3

STANFORD PIONEER

When Bert Hoover arrived at Stanford University in the summer of 1891, he saw only a group of unfinished buildings set on a dusty former hayfield. Palo Alto, California, the town that surrounds the university today, did not yet exist. He moved into a boardinghouse and waited for the men's dormitory to be completed.

As workers rushed to finish the university's construction, Bert got ready for a second try at his entrance examination. He was coached by the two schoolteachers who ran the boardinghouse. In return for their help, he took care of their horses, a job he had learned while living with the Minthorns.

After many hours of study, Bert passed his tests in all but one subject—English grammar. School officials offered to overlook this weakness if Bert would correct it before graduation. However, the officials also discovered that he was still one subject short of meeting the entrance requirements. Bert decided to try the test in physiology, even though he had never taken the course in school.

Those long buggy rides with Dr. Minthorn to see patients now paid off. The knowledge Bert had gained on these trips helped him pass the physiology test after just two days of study. Thus, the school dropout became a Stanford "pioneer." This was the name the university gave to the students who formed its first class.

Once settled in, Bert needed to find a job. Although students did not have to pay for classes, they had to buy textbooks and pay for their room and board in the dormitory. Besides the two hundred ten dollars brought from Oregon, all Bert had was six hundred dollars left in his college fund, which his guardian was holding in Iowa. With Professor Swain's help, Bert got a job in a college office. He also continued to care for the boardinghouse horses twice a day.

Bert declared his field of study to be mechanical engineering. However, after Professor John Branner arrived in early 1892 to set up a geology department, Bert enrolled in a class in geology, the study of the earth's composition. Dr. Branner was impressed with this eager young freshman, and Bert soon became his favorite student.[1] "So many [students] fumble assignments," Branner noted. "But I can tell Hoover to do a thing and never think of it again."[2]

Learning of Bert's financial problems, Professor

Branner hired him as the geology office assistant. Here, too, Hoover impressed Branner with his ability to organize tasks, and pay attention to detail.[3]

At the end of Bert's freshman year, Branner got him a summer job helping with a study of the Ozark Mountains in Arkansas. It offered practical experience and paid a much-needed forty dollars a month. Like Professor Branner, Hoover's boss in Arkansas was impressed by his efficiency and energy.[4]

Over the summer, hard work in the mountainous terrain changed Bert into a fit and muscular young man. By summer's end, he had saved an additional sixty dollars for his education. He also witnessed widespread poverty for the first time. Hoover later described the living conditions of many Ozark families as "horrible." He was especially troubled by the effects of poor diets on the mountain children.[5]

When he returned to Stanford for his second year, Bert officially changed his field of study from engineering to geology. He continued to assist Professor Branner throughout his college years. He added to his income at various times by operating a student laundry service, running a campus concert and lecture series, and starting a campus paper route. Summers found him again at work on government geology projects, mainly in the mountains of California and Nevada. It was here that Hoover became interested in the mining industry.[6]

Although Bert was energetic, hardworking, and ambitious, his academic record at Stanford was not outstanding. Even in his senior year, he continued to struggle with English grammar. He was able to graduate only because a science professor corrected the spelling and punctuation errors on his final English paper before he handed it in.

One Stanford professor later remembered that Hoover's strength had not been his schoolwork, but his ability to organize and run campus affairs.[7] Bert left his mark on the university as a "doer" rather than a thinker. "Do your work so that they notice it and be on the job all the time," he once advised a fellow student.[8]

Bert followed his own advice. In addition to his jobs and businesses, he organized the school's Geology Club and headed it for much of his college career. He took charge of the student store and reorganized it so that it made a profit. In his junior year, Hoover was elected class treasurer. He wiped out a two thousand-dollar class debt and set up a system to prevent financial fraud. He also wrote the student constitution.

Bert also played on Stanford's baseball team. However, he decided he would prefer to manage the team. Here, too, he organized events to run smoothly and correctly. One time, former president Benjamin Harrison visited the campus. When a gatekeeper admitted the great man to a baseball game for free, Hoover confronted him and demanded that he buy a ticket.[9]

Eventually, Hoover became financial manager for all Stanford athletics. Once, when a football player asked for new shoes, Bert demanded to see the old ones first. "What you need is a pair of new laces," he noted, and laces were all he would provide.[10] Such behavior did not win Hoover many friends. However, he was more concerned with getting results than with being popular.

Nineteen-year-old Herbert Hoover is standing second from the left in this 1893 photo of Stanford University's first geology class.

Bert's college years strengthened the teachings of his Quaker upbringing. Among these were that a person should be productive and that life is meant for accomplishment. "Men and women are judged by achievements, not by dreams," advised Stanford's president at the time.[11] However, Stanford's greatest single influence on Hoover turned out to be neither an accomplishment nor an idea. Instead, it was a person.

One day in Bert's senior year, Professor Branner asked his assistant to explain some rock samples to a new student, Lou Henry. Bert was dazzled by this tall, attractive freshman who had just become the school's first female geology student. He later joked about their initial meeting:

> As I was Dr. Branner's handy boy in the department, I felt it my duty to aid the young lady in her studies both in the laboratory and in the field. . . . And this call to

duty was stimulated by her whimsical mind, her blue eyes, and a broad, grinnish smile.[12]

Bert quickly learned that he and Lou had much in common beyond their interest in geology. Both had been born in Iowa and had come west during their childhood. Lou was from Monterey, California, where her father was a banker. Raised by this man who wanted sons, she had learned to camp and fish. Like Bert, she had a great love for the outdoors. Lou also shared Bert's strong sense of independence and self-reliance. "It isn't so important what others think of you," she told another student, "as what you feel inside yourself."[13]

Within a week of their first meeting, Hoover asked Lou for a date. Her friends, many of whom knew Bert as their laundry collector, advised her against seeing him socially. But she accepted the invitation anyway. It marked the beginning of a loving and loyal relationship that would last half a century.

In May 1895, Herbert Hoover took his place alongside the other remaining "pioneers" as part of Stanford University's first graduating class. His geology degree in hand, he began to look for a job. He decided that his best chance of finding one was in the California mountains where he had worked the previous two summers. So while Lou continued her studies at Stanford, Bert headed for the goldfields. There he hoped to find a professional position with a mining company.

Getting a job in 1895 was easier said than done. The nation was in the midst of a severe depression. Hoover soon discovered that there were more job seekers than jobs. In addition, most mine bosses were not impressed

Lou Henry works on an assignment in Stanford's chemistry lab. She was beginning her studies at the university while Hoover was completing his. The two met at about the time this photo was taken.

by a well-dressed young man with a college degree. "Get in there and dig," one told him. "You need a nose for gold. It can't be learned by sticking your nose in a book. You'll develop it by working where the gold is."[14]

Living in a run-down hotel in Nevada City, California, and with his money nearly gone, Hoover lowered his expectations. He took a laborer's job on the night shift, deep inside a mine. After a miner filled a cart with ore, Bert had to push it along a dark, damp tunnel to the mine's vertical shaft, where it was hoisted to the surface. It was dirty and tiring work for which he earned fourteen dollars for a week of seven ten-hour days.

Even this miserable job was not secure during those hard economic times. After a few weeks, the mine's production slowed, and Hoover was let go. He reported, "I then learned what the bottom levels of real human despair were paved with. . . the ceaseless tramping and ceaseless refusal at the employment office day by day."[15]

Finally, Bert was hired for the night shift at another mine. His new boss called him "the professor," a nickname that made his acceptance by the other miners more difficult. Still, these uneducated men taught the young college graduate the basics of mining.

By Christmas, Bert decided that he had seen enough of a miner's life. His education had prepared him for something better than working like a mule, he told a friend. Hoover now had both money in savings and practical mining experience. So in early 1896 he went to San Francisco to seek a professional position.[16]

In San Francisco, Bert was reunited with his brother and sister. Tad had quit college after Grandmother Minthorn died. He was working to support sister Mary, now a high school student, who had come to live with him. Tad and Mary invited Bert to stay with them. For the first time since their mother's death, the Hoover children were under one roof. The move also brought Bert back to Lou. Stanford was just a few miles away.

Bert found that professional mining jobs in San Francisco were as scarce as they had been in the goldfields. So again he lowered his expectations. He took a job as office boy for Louis Janin, the top mining engineer in the city.

In his typical style, Bert soon showed himself to be a valuable employee. Janin had been hired by a mining company as an expert witness in an important lawsuit. Hoover prepared the maps, data, and other evidence that helped win the case. Janin rewarded Bert by making the young man his assistant. Then he assigned Hoover to help manage a client's mine in New Mexico.

After a few months in the field, Janin called Hoover back to work in the office. Once more Bert lived with Tad and Mary, and he resumed his trips to Stanford to visit Lou. However, Bert's stay in San Francisco was again brief. His hard work and talent soon brought a wonderful opportunity.

A British company had asked Janin to find an American who could develop mines in Australia. A gold rush had just begun there. The job paid five thousand dollars a year, a good salary for the times. The company wanted an experienced professional who was at least thirty-five years old. Janin recommended Bert Hoover anyway, and although he was only twenty-two, he got the job. Little did the young man suspect the adventures that awaited him!

4

THE GLOBETROTTER

May 1897 found Herbert Hoover in western Australia. Gold fever was high, and people traveled great distances to find the precious ore. However, few of the world's mining regions were more remote.

The region received only about an inch of rainfall a year. The air was full of dust. Temperatures seldom dropped below one hundred degrees, even at night. The land of "sin, sand, sweat, sorrow [and] sore eyes," the locals called it.[1] Hoover learned to bathe in beer because water was so scarce and expensive. "Every man here talks of when to go home," he wrote to a friend. "None come to stay except those who die."[2]

As he had so many times before, Hoover made the best of his situation and worked tirelessly. He sometimes remained inside the sweltering tin shack that was his office—working and planning —until 3 A.M. He made repeated expeditions hundreds of miles into the scorching countryside. There he inspected the company's mines and searched for other opportunities.

Hoover's efforts brought him more success. On one of his trips, he came upon a small mine owned by a rival company. His training in geology led him to believe that these miners were working a huge vein of gold. He also suspected they did not know the true value of their holdings. So he recommended to his British employer, Bewick, Moreing & Company, that they risk five hundred thousand dollars to purchase and develop this mine.

Bewick, Moreing made Bert the mine's manager and gave him a share of its profits. Over the next fifty years, the mine produced $65 million in earnings. In fact, due largely to Hoover's efforts, Bewick, Moreing was one of the few mining companies to show a profit during the Australian gold rush.

To reward Hoover, the company raised his yearly salary to $12,500. However, he was becoming increasingly unhappy about his life in Australia. "Anyone who envies me my salary can just take my next trip with me," Hoover wrote. "He will then be contented to be a bank clerk at $3 a week the rest of his life, just to live in the United States."[3]

Lou Henry probably played a large part in Hoover's homesickness. In June 1898, she completed her studies at Stanford. Like Hoover, she graduated with a degree in geology. The two were not officially engaged, but before he left for Australia, they had reached an "understanding." Hoover was now financially secure and successful professionally. It seemed a good time to do something about his personal life.

So in late 1898, when Bewick, Moreing asked Hoover to take on a series of assignments in China, he reacted by sending two telegrams. The first was to his company, accepting the job on the condition that he could visit the United States first. The second went to Lou Henry, asking her to marry him and go with him to China. Lou said yes.

On February 10, 1899, Herbert Hoover and Lou Henry were married at the Henry family home in Monterey. The next day, the newlyweds sailed for Tientsin, a major seaport in northern China. There Hoover faced some challenging tasks. He was to improve the city's harbor and port facilities. He would help develop Chinese mining in a nation where the industry was controlled by foreign companies. Most important, he was to protect his employer's investments during the political crisis that was plaguing China. For seeing to these three jobs, he would be paid a total of twenty thousand dollars a year.

For more than fifty years, powerful nations had been taking advantage of China's weakness, forcing harsh treaties on that country. Great Britain, France, Russia, Germany, Japan, and other countries had established what amounted to colonies in China. Within these areas, they controlled industry, natural resources, transportation, and trade. While the foreigners became rich, China benefited little.

In the late 1890s, some Chinese began plotting to

Lou Henry and Herbert Hoover pose with Lou's father (rear left), mother (faint, far right) and sister (left, front) outside the Henry home on their wedding day in February 1899. Lou is directly behind Bert.

regain control of their country. Not wanting to risk war with the occupying nations, China's empress did not openly side with these Chinese patriots. However, she secretly supported their goals.

Tension was high when Herbert and Lou Hoover arrived in Tientsin in March 1899. But as he had so often done before, Hoover worked hard to carry out his mission. To help the government find and develop its own natural resources, he made many trips into China's vast countryside. On others, he inspected mines in which Bewick, Moreing had invested. Sometimes he was gone for weeks at a time. Lou Hoover, who was also a licensed mining engineer, went with him on some of these expeditions.

Because of growing antiforeign feelings, Hoover's trips were escorted by government officials and protected by Chinese troops. However, most of the Chinese Hoover met treated him well. Perhaps this was because rumors had it that his green eyes could see into the ground and find gold.[4]

Yet forces were at work in China that not even Herbert Hoover could overcome. In early 1900, a radical group calling itself *I Ho Tuan*, literally meaning "righteous harmonious fists," began a violent campaign to drive all foreigners out of the country. English-speaking reporters translated the group's name as the "Boxers." Their uprising became known as the Boxer Rebellion. China's army was unable—or unwilling—to restore order.

As the Boxer Rebellion swept northward, Hoover called his workers in from the field. He and Lou returned to their home in Tientsin. About twenty-five hundred troops from several European nations arrived in the city. China's government also sent soldiers and some artillery to protect the foreigners. With the seven hundred other civilians who were living in Tientsin's foreign section, the Hoovers hoped they would be safe.[5]

When the Boxers arrived, however, the Chinese troops refused to fight. Some army units even turned their artillery pieces over to the Boxers and joined them. Using these big guns, the Boxers began to bombard the foreigners in early June.

Learning that Hoover was an engineer, the Russian

SOURCE DOCUMENT

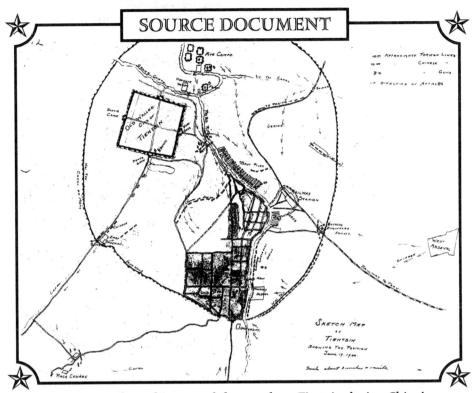

Lou Hoover drew this map of the attack on Tientsin during China's Boxer Rebellion of 1900. The shaded area is the foreign section where the Hoovers lived and which they helped defend.

in command of the foreign troops asked him to build defenses. Bert quickly organized the foreigners and about one thousand Christian Chinese, who had fled to the foreign section. Overnight they erected barricades, using sacks of rice, sugar, and peanuts that were in the city's warehouses.

From behind these walls, the foreigners held off twenty-five thousand Boxers and five thousand Chinese troops for almost thirty days. During the ordeal, the Boxers fired thousands of artillery shells into the foreign section. Rifle bullets whizzed through the air, day and night. About three hundred people inside the settlement were killed.

Hoover worked tirelessly. He helped fight fires caused by the shelling. He was also among those who sneaked out at night to get water for the settlement. Hoover showed little concern for his safety, once running through a hail of bullets to save a little Chinese girl.

Lou Hoover was also brave, but she was more careful. "She became expert at riding her bicycle close to the walls of buildings to avoid stray bullets and shells," Hoover recalled later. "One day she had a tire punctured by a bullet."[6]

Lou Hoover poses next to a cannon protecting the foreign section of Tientsin, China, during the Boxer Rebellion. Lou carried a gun and stood guard at these defenses, which were designed by her husband.

Finally, on July 13, a force of Japanese, American, and British troops arrived and drove the Boxers off. That night Hoover sent a one-word telegram to Lou's father in California—"Safe."[7] With their defeat at Tientsin, the Boxers were crushed.

The next month, Bert and Lou Hoover sailed for England. In his pocket was a paper transferring control of a rich mining area to Bewick, Moreing. Hoover and his employer had helped a Chinese company develop the mines there. Chinese officials feared that the Russians in China might seize these mines as punishment for the Boxer Rebellion. By turning control over to the British company that was helping them, the Chinese hoped to keep the Russians from taking the mines.[8]

In January 1901, Hoover returned to China as general manager of Bewick, Moreing's new holdings. At once he was faced with problems. Just as the Chinese had feared, the Russians had, in fact, interfered and hauled off the mines' equipment. In addition, the Japanese had seized the mining company's offices in Tientsin. In all, Hoover had to negotiate with the governments of five nations to get the mines running again.

No sooner were these problems settled than a group of Belgians demanded control of the mines. They had quietly bought up enough stock from Chinese and other investors to gain ownership of the properties. Soon a new mine manager arrived. Hoover, who was irate, quit his job and made plans to return to America.[9]

To keep their star employee, the owners of Bewick, Moreing offered Hoover a share of their company. It was a fantastic deal, especially for a man just twenty-seven years old. They promised him $12,500 a year, 20 percent of the company's profits, and $250,000 in company stock. In addition, he would be able to work from the company's headquarters in London, England. Hoover quickly accepted the offer.

For the next seven years, the Hoovers lived in London. There, in 1903, the couple's first child, Herbert Jr., was born. Hoover, however, spent most of his time traveling, inspecting mines that Bewick, Moreing owned, managed, or advised all over the world. Lou and Bert Jr. went with him on many of these journeys.

During his travels, Hoover had many adventures. In Egypt, his workers unearthed an ancient ruin in a turquoise mine. Scientists were able to learn much more about the history of ancient Egypt from this discovery. On another occasion, Bert and a helper were exploring an abandoned mine in Burma when, armed only with candles, they came across a tiger living in one of the tunnels. "The tiger, fortunately, . . . did not come out to greet us," Hoover later wrote in his memoirs.[10] While in Burma, Bert came down with malaria. This deadly disease causes high fevers and loss of touch with reality. It was months before he fully recovered.

In 1908 Hoover decided to leave Bewick, Moreing. He blamed the decision on his health problems, but he had other reasons. He and his wife were both eager to go back home to the United States. A second son, Allan, had been born in 1907, and they wanted their children to attend American schools.[11]

Due largely to Hoover, Bewick, Moreing's business had tripled by 1908. The sale of his interest in the company provided him with a $169,000 profit. Income from mines in which he had a share also added to his substantial wealth.

At just thirty-four years old, Hoover was already one of the world's best—and best-paid—mining engineers. Yet he was not satisfied. He had developed some very original ideas about his profession. Hoover wanted to go far beyond what were "normal" engineering practices at the time, and he hoped to do so by starting his own company.

In Hoover's mind, engineering was a step-by-step approach to solving problems. An engineer's first task, he believed, was to see whether the problem was even worth solving. The next steps were to study the problem, then come up with a general way of dealing with it. After that, detailed plans for attacking the problem should be made. Only after these preliminary steps were completed should the engineer actually try to solve the problem.[12]

This was not a common way of thinking in the early 1900s. Most people did not take such a "scientific" approach. However, Hoover followed his engineering principles for the rest of his life. He applied them to almost any problem he had, including the challenges he faced later, during his years in government.

In July 1908, Hoover launched his new firm. For the next six years, he was even busier than he had been at Bewick, Moreing. He became known as an engineering "doctor" who could make "sick" companies profitable again. If improvement was possible, Hoover cured the "patient" almost every time. The Herbert Hoover

Company had offices in New York, San Francisco, London, Paris, and Petrograd, Russia. Among his employees were some top engineers whom he had lured away from Bewick, Moreing. He also brought his brother into the business. With Bert's financial help and advice, Tad Hoover had also completed an engineering degree at Stanford.

By 1914, Herbert Hoover was at the height of his

Lou Henry Hoover relaxes with her sons, nine-year-old Bert Jr. (left) and Allan (right), age five, in 1912.

career. His ability and hard work had brought him to head a company and mines that employed one hundred seventy-five thousand people around the globe. He had spread American machinery, mining methods, and culture worldwide. He was well known on four continents. It is estimated that between 1901 and 1914, Hoover spent time in nearly forty countries.

His financial success was also assured. By 1910 he was earning $100,000 a year. "If a man has not made a million dollars by the time he is forty, he's not worth much," Hoover said in 1907.[13] In 1914, on the eve of his fortieth birthday, he was worth about $4 million.

Yet despite his successes, Herbert Hoover wanted something more. "Just making money isn't enough," he told a friend.[14] As he became tired of mining engineering, he searched for new challenges. He began to donate time and money to Stanford University. In 1912, Hoover was named to the board that oversaw the school. He briefly considered becoming Stanford's president. He also thought about buying some newspapers and starting a new career in publishing.[15]

Hoover even considered retiring. But to him, retirement meant only the end of working for pay. His Quaker upbringing had taught him the importance of accomplishing something that was useful to the world.[16] "It is up to every man to do a service for his country when it can be done," he said.[17]

As Hoover debated what to do next, events were taking place that helped him make his decision. In 1914, an assassin's bullet that was fired in Europe created the opportunity he had been looking for.

5

FOOD REGULATOR OF THE WORLD

In June 1914, the heir to the throne of Austria-Hungary was killed by an assassin. Austria-Hungary blamed its neighbor Serbia for the act. Within weeks the two countries went to war. The United States remained neutral. That is, it did not take either side. But treaties pulled other nations into what is now called World War I.

Russia was pledged to defend Serbia. It was also allied with Great Britain and France. Austria-Hungary's ally was Germany. To attack northern France, Germany invaded neutral Belgium, which lay between. In just six days, Europe was at war.

The speed of these events caught Americans in Europe by surprise. Most fled to London. There they hoped to buy tickets on ships bound for the United

States. Because of the crisis, however, the British government had closed the banks. Unable to cash checks, thousands of Americans were broke and stranded. (There were no credit cards or ATM machines in the early 1900s.) Many did not even have money for food.

Herbert Hoover was in London on business as the crisis unfolded. In early August, United States officials in Great Britain asked him to help send all the stranded Americans home. "I did not realize it at the moment, but . . . my engineering career was over," he recalled later. "I [now] was on the slippery road of public life."[1]

For the next several weeks, Hoover worked painstakingly to coordinate the relief effort. Some five hundred volunteers collected and distributed clothing and money to the needy Americans in England. More than $1.5 million was raised. More than one hundred twenty thousand Americans were served.

Hoover was proud of this accomplishment. But he was troubled that his private effort was more efficient and less expensive than the United States government's official aid program, which began about two weeks later. This comparison weakened his confidence in government's ability to help people with their problems.[2]

In mid-October, as Herbert and Lou prepared to return to America, a group of Belgians contacted the Hoovers. They related a terrible story of suffering in their country.

A small and densely populated country, Belgium produced less than half the food it needed. For the rest, it depended on imports from other nations. However, Germany's invasion in early August had destroyed

Belgian farms and crops. It also had disrupted Belgium's trade. The Hoovers' Belgian visitors predicted that millions of people in their country would starve unless a program was started to feed its citizens. They told Hoover that he was the ideal person for this task.[3]

Because Hoover was a neutral American, the Germans would allow him to operate in Belgium. In addition, his travels as a mining engineer had made him a well-known figure. He would get cooperation from world leaders that a lesser-known person might not. His engineering work had also given him experience in organizing and managing large international projects.

Hoover thought over the Belgians' request. He knew he would have to give up his engineering work if he accepted their mission. Feeding an entire country would be a huge effort, especially during a war. Finally, he accepted the challenge with two conditions: He wanted no pay, and he demanded complete control over the project.[4] He instructed his brother, Tad, to sell his mining engineering business.

The private aid group that Hoover organized became known as the Commission for Relief in Belgium, or CRB. The job he faced was immense. Sources of food had to be found throughout the world. Money had to be raised to buy it. Then the food had to be delivered safely past the armies and navies of warring nations. Finally, it had to be distributed fairly and in a way that did not help Belgium's German conquerors.

For the next two-and-a-half years, Hoover coordinated this relief effort. He worked twelve to eighteen hours a day. In 1915, he expanded the aid program to include the people of war-torn northern France. By the time World War I ended in 1918, his program of food aid had kept more than 10 million people from starving.

Hoover bought corn from Argentina, rice in Burma, and Chinese beans. American farmers sold him wheat and meat. The CRB's food purchases averaged about one hundred fifty thousand tons a month. To move all this food, Hoover hired entire railroad trains and fleets of ships. The CRB even operated its own flour mills, bakeries, and food-processing plants. Eventually, the aid program provided clothing as well.

The cost of these activities was tremendous. At its height, the CRB required about $25 million a month to operate. Because the relief effort was not a government program, this money had to come from voluntary donations. Committees were set up all over the world to raise these funds.

Many problems threatened the program. Despite promises of safe passage, German submarines sank CRB ships. The Germans accused some United States relief workers of spying and expelled them from Belgium. Sometimes they seized the Belgians' food for themselves. The British Navy threatened to prevent CRB ships from reaching Belgium. British leaders thought Hoover's program was helping the enemy. In part, this was because CRB aid freed Germany from the responsibility of having to take care of the people its armies had recently conquered.

In early 1917, Germany announced that its submarines would attack all ships they met on the high seas. The merchant ships of neutral nations were

Workers in Belgium distribute food provided by Hoover's European relief organization during the early years of World War I.

included in this threat. This policy was a clear violation of American neutrality. So in April 1917, the United States declared war on Germany. President Woodrow Wilson asked Hoover to return to America to manage the nation's wartime food supply.

The Hoover family arrived in Washington, D.C., in May 1917. In just a few days Bert set up the United States Food Administration. As he had at the CRB, Hoover accepted no pay and demanded complete control. He recruited some of his top assistants from the CRB to help him.

The United States troops that would soon be battling

the Germans in Europe had to be fed. America's new allies, Great Britain and France, also needed more food. Hoover's challenge was to supply all these groups overseas and still have enough food left for Americans at home. "The outcome of the war," he said, "may depend upon what we can produce, as well as what we can save."[5]

Hoover insisted that the food program be voluntary. He did not want the government to tell farmers what and how much they could produce. He rejected the idea of rationing, or allowing Americans only limited amounts of foods that were greatly needed overseas.[6] Hoover revealed his approach in an announcement to the American people. It was a policy he would follow again later, during the crisis that would plague him as president:

> The whole foundation of democracy lies in the individual initiative [effort] of its people and their willingness to serve the interests of the nation . . . in the time of emergency. I hold that democracy can yield to discipline and that we can solve this food problem for our own people and for our allies largely by voluntary action.[7]

Even the Food Administration itself was largely a volunteer organization. Only eight thousand of the agency's workers were government employees, and these were mostly clerks. Its programs were carried out by about seven hundred fifty thousand unpaid volunteers across the country.

To conserve food, Hoover created "meatless Mondays" and "wheatless Wednesdays." People were asked to eat fish instead of beef, or vegetables for bread on these days. Food preparers were urged to serve smaller portions and to use all leftovers.

Food Administration volunteers went door-to-door to ask families to sign pledge cards, promising to follow these guidelines. Some 20 million did so and received window stickers to show they were "doing their part" to win the war.

To get farmers to produce more of certain foods, Hoover offered financial encouragements. He guaranteed farmers high prices for wheat, beef, and other products that were needed for United States troops or by America's allies. He also urged the farmers to produce more food of all kinds.

Behind all the methods to gain the nation's cooperation with the food program was a strong appeal to patriotism. "Food Will Win the War!" appeared on Food Administration banners and posters everywhere.

The Food Administration's program was one of the greatest successes of the war. By the time Germany surrendered in October 1918, about 220 million people in allied and neutral countries had been fed by American food sent to Europe.

After World War I, President Woodrow Wilson asked Hoover to stay on in government. He wanted Hoover to organize a program to aid all of Europe. Much of the continent had been devastated by more than four years of fighting. About 400 million Europeans needed food, clothing, or medical supplies.

Communists had seized power in Russia during the war. Communism is a system in which the government owns all land and businesses for the people. There is no

A volunteer in Mobile, Alabama, puts up a Food Administration poster urging residents to do their patriotic duty. Hoover managed the nation's food conservation effort during World War I.

private ownership and no free enterprise under this system. Wilson feared that the great suffering that followed the war would now cause people of other countries to turn to communism. He asked Hoover to help Europeans survive until they could plant and harvest new crops.[8]

Hoover combined the activities of the CRB and the Food Administration into the American Relief Administration. In December 1918, with a few key assistants from Washington, he set up headquarters in Paris, France. For another ten months, Hoover continued the exhausting schedule he had begun in 1914. When asked about Hoover's activities, General John Pershing, the commander of American forces in Europe, replied: "Mr. Hoover is the food regulator of the world."[9]

About four thousand American troops and volunteers helped run Hoover's program. So did thousands of workers in the countries being helped. To speed the arrival of aid, Hoover asked that United States troop ships coming to Europe to bring home American soldiers be filled with relief supplies. The United States Army in Europe turned over all its extra food and clothing to Hoover for distribution to needy Europeans.

Any European nation that cooperated with the American aid workers was eligible for assistance. Over the bitter objections of some European leaders, Hoover included Germany and other former World War I enemy nations in the relief effort. To calm America's allies, he put the Friends Service Committee, a Quaker organization, in charge of the aid program in Germany.

As had been the case in Belgium a few years before, Hoover was especially concerned about the children. His own experience as an orphan had made him extra-sensitive to their plight. All over Europe, millions of young people lived in horrible conditions because of the effects of the war. Hoover set up programs to make sure all children got one hot meal a day. Orphans and homeless youth were given shelter and three meals daily.[10]

As America's relief efforts drew to a close, Europeans honored the man whose long service, continuous work, and unwavering dedication had helped so many. Cities named streets and parks after him. Hoover became an honorary citizen of Belgium, Finland, and Poland.

In September 1919, Herbert Hoover came home. His

Herbert Hoover (far right) visits the docks in Brooklyn, New York, to personally supervise loading relief supplies on ships bound for Europe after World War I.

job was done. On the lengthy ocean voyage, he had time to reflect on just what he had accomplished. His relief program had, in only twelve months, distributed nearly $6 billion in food, seed, clothing, and supplies to more than twenty nations. It had saved millions from starvation. Hoover believed that he had helped keep large parts of Europe from falling prey to communism. In addition, at least 15 million children had been restored to good health.[11]

The voyage home was Hoover's first real chance to rest in more than five years. The wartime emergency was over. He looked forward to returning to private life at last. However, that was not to be.

6

THE WONDER BOY

H erbert Hoover returned to California "hoping that I had served my turn in public life and might now devote myself to a reasonable existence."[1] With Lou and the boys, he took a rest. They camped and fished in the mountains of the west. Then he prepared to resume his engineering career.

Because of his nomadic lifestyle, at age forty-five Hoover had never actually owned a home. Now the Hoovers built a house on a hill overlooking Stanford University. For Lou, the house was a symbol of the quiet, settled life she hoped would follow.[2] "My ambition is to get out of the limelight as fast as possible," Bert told friends.[3] However, his widespread popularity quickly shattered those plans.

Between October 1919 and March 1921, Hoover

made forty-six speeches. He also wrote fifty-nine magazine articles and press statements, chaired fifteen conferences, and testified before Congress nine times. In addition, he helped several groups that were involved in public service. Hoover complained that instead of his new house, his real home was a railroad car.[4]

A public opinion poll in 1920 named Hoover one of the nation's ten most important people.[5] Both the Democratic and the Republican parties asked him to run for president.

Hoover had no interest in any elected office in 1920. During the war some people had criticized the way he managed the programs he headed. He was angered that

Lou and Herbert Hoover built this magnificent house in Palo Alto, following their return to California after World War I. However, they spent most of the rest of their lives in Washington, D.C., and New York City.

anyone would question his methods or doubt that he was right. However, when Republican Warren Harding became president in 1921, Hoover accepted his offer to be the new secretary of commerce.

Today, the Department of Commerce has many functions. Chief among them is serving the nation's businesses. However, when Hoover became its head, it was only a minor government agency. A former secretary of commerce told Hoover that his job would take only two hours a day to do, but Hoover saw new opportunities in the position.

The nation had economic problems in the years after World War I. The government no longer needed food, supplies, and equipment for the military. In addition, just as factories and farms started to produce less, thousands of ex-soldiers were looking for work. Hoover thought he could help rebuild the American economy in much the same way he had helped rebuild Europe after the war.

One of the Commerce Department's main functions was to conduct the census. This is the population count the government makes every ten years. Hoover believed the data the Census Bureau collected could be useful to businesses in their planning. Within months after he took over, the department began to publish monthly statistics about industrial production and trade.

Before Hoover, the department's Bureau of Standards merely tested products the government was about to buy. Hoover turned the bureau into the world's largest research laboratory. He offered its services to help businesses solve complex problems. He also directed it to develop safety and product standards.

Hoover believed that by making too many sizes and versions of certain products, industries were not operating efficiently. As manufacturers began to realize his ideas could save them money, they began to ask for help in this area. Under Hoover's guidance, the Commerce Department developed standard sizes for paper, automobile tires, nuts and bolts, lightbulbs, and many more products. Hoover knew this standardization would lower costs and ultimately make products more available to the people. The department also issued safety standards for car brakes, elevators, building cement, and other items.

In carrying out these activities, Hoover was applying to economic life principles learned as a mining engineer and food regulator. A newspaper reporter wrote: "Hoover has regarded our entire business structure as a single factory, conceiving [thinking] himself . . . consulting engineer for the whole enterprise."[6]

Hoover's actions soon made him the second most powerful member of President Harding's Cabinet. Vice-President Calvin Coolidge privately mocked Hoover, sarcastically calling him "Wonder Boy."[7] Nevertheless, when Coolidge became president after Harding's death in 1923, he asked Hoover to remain in the Cabinet. Hoover continued to expand his department and worked to improve the nation's economy.

Hoover persuaded Congress to give his department control of the U.S. Patent Office, recognizing its importance to economic growth.[8] This agency keeps track of new products and new technology. Radio was a new industry in the 1920s, but Hoover knew that it would not succeed without some control. Later, in 1927, his department began licensing radio stations to operate.

Although airplanes were in their infancy in the 1920s, Hoover believed they, too, would be important in the future. In 1926, his department created rules and regulations for air travel. In three years it tripled the number of lighted runways. It also improved navigation and weather equipment. Through these actions, Hoover helped the aviation industry develop.

In the spring of 1927, Hoover returned briefly to organizing relief programs. Much of the Mississippi River valley was hit by a huge flood. Millions of dollars' worth of crops, livestock, and property were destroyed. More than a million people fled their homes. President Coolidge sent Hoover to coordinate relief efforts. Once again, he made front-page news.

Both Hoover's flood relief and the nation's economic growth convinced many Americans that he truly was a wonder boy. By the late 1920s the economy was booming. Most people enjoyed a level of wealth they had never known before. Wages increased. Many people were able to buy homes and cars, to attend sports events, and to travel on vacations for the first time. Americans called these good times the "Roaring Twenties." Hoover played a major role in the nation's economic growth in this period.

During Hoover's eight years at the Commerce Department, his two teenage boys became men. Both attended first a private Quaker school in Washington, D.C., then Palo Alto High School near Stanford in California. During the summers, the older son, Bert Jr.,

President Calvin Coolidge (left) meets with Secretary of Commerce Herbert Hoover at Coolidge's vacation retreat in 1928.

worked at hard physical labor, just as his father had done. He graduated from Stanford University in 1925 and began a career as an electrical engineer. Allan enrolled at Stanford the year his brother graduated.

In 1928, Coolidge decided not to seek another term. Herbert Hoover was the Republican's logical choice for president. Few shared Hoover's own inner doubts about whether his shyness and stubbornness would prevent him from being effective in public elective office. However, he did not even have to campaign for his party's nomination. "Who but Hoover?" millions of Americans asked.[9]

In June, the Republican party named Hoover as its candidate for president. He was just short of his fifty-fourth birthday. In accepting the nomination, Hoover stated his faith in the nation he had so tirelessly and successfully served:

> My country . . . . gave me, as it gives every boy and girl, a chance. . . . In no other land could a boy from a country village, without inheritance or influential friends, look forward with such unbounded hope. My whole life has taught me what America means. I am indebted to my country beyond any human power to repay.[10]

That same month the Democratic party chose Al Smith as its candidate.

Rarely have two presidential candidates offered voters such a clear-cut choice. Hoover came from the west. Smith was from the east. Hoover grew up in rural America. Smith, the son of Irish immigrants, had been raised in New York City. This was Hoover's first election campaign. Smith had worked his way up though various elective offices to become governor of New York.

In 1919, the Eighteenth Amendment to the Constitution had outlawed the manufacture and sale of alcoholic beverages in the United States. Hoover supported this policy, which was called "Prohibition." Smith favored its repeal.

Smith was also the first Catholic to run for president. Many Republicans and other Hoover supporters charged that if Smith were elected, the Pope would rule the nation. Such personal attacks angered Hoover. He strongly condemned them in the first speech of his campaign:

I come of Quaker stock. My ancestors were persecuted for their beliefs. . . . By blood and conviction, I stand for religious tolerance. . . . The glory of our American ideals is the right of every man to worship God according to his own conscience.[11]

In 1928, presidential campaigns were shorter than they are today. Hoover made only seven speeches. Uncomfortable in crowds, he was the first president to depend mainly on radio to reach the American people. His message emphasized how the nation had prospered

SOURCE DOCUMENT

One of the oldest and perhaps the noblest of human aspirations has been the abolition of poverty. By poverty I mean the grinding by undernourishment, cold, and ignorance, and fear of old age of those who have the will to work. We in America today are nearer to the final triumph over poverty than ever before in the history of any land. The poorhouse is vanishing from among us. Given a chance to go forward with the policies of the last 8 years, we shall soon with the help of God be in sight of the day when poverty will be banished from this Nation. There is no guarantee against poverty equal to a job for every man. That is the primary purpose of the economic policies we advocate. . . .

Our purpose is to build in this Nation a human society, not an economic system. We wish to increase the efficiency and productivity of our country, but its final purpose is happier homes. We shall succeed through the faith, the loyalty, the self-sacrifice, the devotion to eternal ideals which live today in every American.

On August 11, 1928, Herbert Hoover delivered the first speech of his presidential campaign at Stanford University. In his speech, Hoover predicted a bright future for the nation.

under Republican leadership. As Will Rogers, the most popular comedian of the 1920s, remarked, "You can't lick this prosperity thing; even the fellow that hasn't got any is all excited over the idea."[12] In the November election, Hoover won in a landslide, capturing 58 percent of the popular vote and winning in forty of the nation's forty-eight states.

Despite his overwhelming victory, Hoover's joy was mixed with concern. He knew that weaknesses existed in the nation's economy. "The American people think me a sort of superman," he said as he awaited Inauguration Day. "They expect the impossible of me and should there arise in the land conditions with which the political machinery is unable to cope, I will be the one to suffer."[13] Hoover's fear was a chilling prediction of the future.

7

GOOD TIMES AND BAD

After the election, Herbert and Lou Hoover began a seven-week tour of Central and South America. Relations with Latin America were not good. For about thirty years, the United States had been involved in the affairs of Central America and the Caribbean. For example, in 1898, the United States had pushed Spain into a war in order to end Spanish control over Cuba. In 1903, President Theodore Roosevelt had helped a revolution in Panama so that the United States could get permission to build the Panama Canal. In 1928, at the time of Hoover's tour, United States Marines were in Haiti and Nicaragua, protecting leaders in nations friendly to America against revolts by their own people.

Many Latin Americans resented the United States'

meddling in their affairs. Hoover assured them that when he became president, the United States would become a "good neighbor." He also pledged to remove United States troops from Latin America. In time, he kept both promises.

On March 4, 1929, Herbert Hoover was inaugurated as the thirty-first president of the United States. For the first time, the nation heard the event over the radio. After taking the oath of office, Hoover told the American people:

> Ours is a land rich in resources . . . filled with millions
> of happy homes, blessed with comfort and opportunity
> . . . . In no nation are the fruits of accomplishment more
> secure. . . . I have no fears for the future of our country.
> It is bright with hope.[1]

As was his practice in all endeavors, Hoover worked very hard at being president. Most days began at 6:00 A.M., as he caught up on his reading. At 7:30 there was a game of "medicine ball" on the White House lawn. This was an activity Hoover invented to lose weight without spending a lot of time at exercise. The game involved two teams throwing a large, eight-pound leather ball over a ten-foot-high net. Besides Hoover, the teams included Cabinet members and their assistants.

Like most first families, the Hoovers entertained frequently. Lou Hoover hired three secretaries to help prepare invitations. However, sometimes things went wrong. Once, five hundred people showed up for a presidential dinner when Mrs. Hoover thought only two hundred had been invited. The White House staff had to hurry out to neighborhood stores for more food.

Lou Hoover took on the job of making the White House into a home. She decorated the living quarters with art and other items that the Hoovers had collected during their years of world travel. For example, a cage of canaries enlivened a second-floor corridor, surrounded by bamboo furniture and grass rugs from South America. At the same time, Mrs. Hoover returned the historic rooms of the White House to their earlier decor. She took special pride in restoring the Lincoln study, which Theodore Roosevelt had made into a children's bedroom, with authentic furniture of Abraham Lincoln's period.

To make the president's office more efficient, Herbert Hoover became the first chief executive to have a telephone on his desk. This amenity allowed him to talk with other government officials quickly and without having to bring them physically to the White House.

One tradition that Hoover viewed as inefficient was the open White House reception. Each day at noon, all Americans who were okayed by the Secret Service could come into the White House to shake the president's hand. Sometimes Hoover had to greet as many as twelve hundred individuals at a single session. He soon ended the practice.

The president not only considered these receptions a waste of valuable time, but he also felt uncomfortable conducting them. He had still not managed to shed the shyness and insecurity of his orphan youth. Later, however, critics would point to the cancellation of these receptions and claim that Hoover did not care about the common people.

Hoover also often avoided the chance to make himself look good. Keeping a low profile was another result of his self-sacrificing upbringing. Once, he tore up a news story one of his backers had written about how he had saved the little Chinese girl during the Boxer Rebellion. On another occasion, he stopped to watch some children playing baseball. After the game, he talked with the children. One of his advisers urged Hoover to return to the baseball field the next day with a photographer. The president refused. Later in his term, Hoover could have used such man-of-the-people publicity.

Hoover began his presidential term with a flurry of reform. One of his early actions was to help the nation's farmers. They had never really recovered from the end of World War I, when Europeans stopped needing American food relief. Hoover worried that if a weakness existed in the nation's prosperity, it would show up most noticeably in rural America.[2]

In June 1929, the president convinced Congress to create a government board to help raise the prices farmers received for their crops. To assist all poor people, he proposed reducing taxes on low-income Americans. He also called for a fifty-dollars-monthly pension for all people over age sixty-five. In addition, continuing the efforts to help children that he had begun during the relief of Belgium, he convened a White House conference on child health and protection.

To help some problem areas of the country, Hoover proposed a series of dams in California and along the Colorado, Tennessee, and Columbia rivers. These projects were intended to provide flood protection, power, and water for irrigation. Construction soon began on the Colorado River near Las Vegas, Nevada, on what was then the world's largest dam. It was named Hoover Dam, in honor of the president. Planning also began for Grand Coulee Dam on the Columbia River in Washington State.

To promote conservation further, Hoover expanded the nation's park system. Two new national parks were added during his term as president. Grand Teton National Park opened in Wyoming, and Great Smoky Mountain National Park opened on the Tennessee-North Carolina border.

Hoover proposed another new national park in the nearby Blue Ridge Mountains of Virginia. With his own money, he bought land in the region and built a retreat that he named Camp Rapidan. Lou Hoover designed and headed the construction of several log cabins that together would house about fifteen guests. Hoover later gave the camp to the new Shenandoah National Park for use by the Boy Scouts and the Girl Scouts. During his four years in the White House he spent many weekends at his retreat, fishing, relaxing, and escaping from the pressures of being president.

Some of these pressures were due to Hoover's clashes with Congress over a number of issues. For example, to improve government efficiency, Hoover expanded the use of civil service in government jobs. Civil service is the system, still used today, that requires workers to be hired on the basis of their qualifications rather than through political connections. Hoover's reforms upset party leaders, who liked to reward loyal Republicans with government jobs.

Another reason for the tensions with Congress had to do with Hoover's personality. In all his previous experiences in public service, Hoover alone had been in charge of his operations. He was not used to sharing power with anyone else, and he had little tolerance for compromise, which is often necessary in politics. "I do not believe that I have the mental attitude or the politician's manner," he once admitted.[3]

Hoover's stubbornness and independence clearly showed in his dealings with Congress. He often insulted its members. Most senators' heads, Hoover said, were nothing but knots that kept their bodies from unraveling.[4] He called one member of Congress "the only verified case of a negative IQ."[5] Legislators found the president equally annoying. "I think he's afraid we senators will influence him," one said. "He doesn't want to get under our influence."[6]

However, there was a more important reason why relations between the president and Congress soured. It was the event that would eventually ruin Hoover's presidency. Eight months into his first year in office, the stock market crashed. This marked the beginning of what later became the worst economic depression in American history.

A "stock market" is the buying and selling of ownership shares, called "stock," in companies. This buying and selling occurs at a place called a "stock exchange." By far, the nation's largest stock exchange was and still is the New York Stock Exchange, located on Wall Street in New York City.

The boom of the 1920s had a huge effect on the stock market. More Americans could afford to buy radios, household goods, automobiles, and other items than ever before. As a result, the value of companies that manufactured or sold such goods went up. When this happened, people wanted to own a part of these companies. So they would buy stock, or their own "share," in companies that appeared to be growing and thriving. This demand for stock in certain companies caused their stock prices to go up even more.

By the late 1920s, however, an unhealthy situation had developed. Because the stock market appeared to be doing so well, many Americans became convinced that stock prices would continue to go up. They began to "speculate," or take a chance that prices would rise quickly. In other words, they stopped buying stock as a long-term investment in a company and instead bought stock in order to make a quick profit by reselling it later at a higher price.

In addition, banks began to loan money to people so that they could buy stock. This enabled many ordinary people who could not otherwise afford to buy stock the opportunity to do so. They, too, wanted to get in on what seemed to be easy profits to be made. Few people worried about what might happen if the value of the stocks ever went down. In the Roaring Twenties, most Americans never believed that was possible.

One who did worry was President Hoover. Even as secretary of commerce, he had been concerned about the stock market's health. He was convinced that many companies' stocks were selling for far more than the companies were really worth. As president, however, Hoover had little power to force a change in stock market practices. He appealed to banks, trying to get them to stop making loans to people for the purpose of buying stock. He also asked New York governor Franklin D. Roosevelt to make the New York Stock Exchange modify some of its practices. Both requests were ignored. In April 1929, concerned about the future of the nation's economic health, Hoover sold many of his own investments.

In October 1929, the event Hoover had been fearing came to pass. Rising interest rates, falling profits, and a number of other complicated economic factors caused stock prices to stop going up. Immediately, some nervous investors on the New York Stock Exchange began to sell their stock. This action caused prices to fall, which prompted other people to sell. In turn, prices dropped even more. The result was more sales and even lower prices. Between October 24 and 28, the value of stock on the New York Stock Exchange plunged about $10 billion. Then, on October 29, 1929, on what commonly became known as Black Tuesday, stock values fell more than $8 billion in a single day. Over the next three weeks, investors in stocks lost more than $30 billion in all.

As the stock market crashed, Americans who had bought stocks with their savings saw all their savings disappear. Worse yet, those who had borrowed money from the bank to buy stock found that their stock was now worth less than what they owed on it. In turn, when these people could not repay their debt, the banks that had made the loans to them suffered huge losses.

Banks use the money that customers, or depositors, put in their savings accounts to make loans to other people. In 1929, banks had loaned out a large portion of their depositors' money to people wanting to speculate in stocks. Now, suddenly, with stock prices falling

---

SOURCE DOCUMENT

Market in Panic as Stocks Are Dumped in 12,894,600 Share Day; Bankers Halt It

Federal Reserve Board Meets, With Secretary Mellon Sitting In, but Announces No Action—Rumors of Rate Cut

TREASURY, HOWEVER, FINDS BASIC CONDITIONS SOUND

Senators Renew Cries in Chorus for Sweeping Investigation of Wall Street Tactics

Outside J. P. Morgan & Co.'s

Richard Whitney's Cry of "205 for Steel" Halts Decline in Record Day's Disorder on Stock Exchange

EXPERTS TERM COLLAPSE SPECULATIVE PHENOMENON

Effect Is Felt on the Curb and Throughout Nation—Financial District Goes Wild

By Elliott Thurston
Special Despatch to The World
WASHINGTON, Oct. 24.—Reassurances from the Treasury that underlying business conditions are sound, an extended but unproductive meeting of the Federal Reserve Board attended by Secretary of the Treasury Mellon, and renewed cries from Capitol Hill for a sweeping investigation of Wall Street, came rapidly in the wake of the stock market debacle.

There were signs that when Secretary Mellon did the rather unusual thing of sitting in with the Federal Reserve Board at a meeting that began when the market closed and lasted for nearly two hours, some sort of statement was to be issued. Gov. Young emerged at the end of the meeting holding what seemed to be the statement, but if it was it had been vetoed. Nothing was said or intimated. The

By Laurence Stern
The stock markets of the country tottered on the brink of panic yesterday as a prosperous people, gone suddenly hysterical with fear, attempted simultaneously to sell a record-breaking volume of securities for whatever they would bring.

The result was a financial nightmare, comparable to nothing ever before experienced in Wall Street. It rocked the financial district to its foundations, hopelessly overwhelmed its mechanical facilities, chilled its blood with terror.

In a society built largely on confidence, with real wealth expressed more or less inaccurately by pieces of paper, the entire fabric of economic stability threatened to come toppling down. Into the frantic hands of a thousand brokers on the floor of the New

The stock market plummet of October 29, 1929, marked the beginning of the Great Depression. Many businesses went bankrupt, and thousands of people lost their jobs.

rapidly, banks started demanding that customers who had taken out loans repay them all at once. However, many customers who had taken out loans were unable to sell the stocks they had bought with the bank loans because their stocks were now nearly worthless. Banks that could not recover these funds were forced to close. When this happened, people who had savings accounts in these banks (whether or not they owed money on loans) lost their money.

Many businesses that could not repay their bank loans were also forced to close. This left their workers without jobs. People who were jobless, or who lost money in the stock market crash, or when their bank closed, bought fewer products. As a result, manufacturers began to produce less goods, causing still more workers to be laid off.

This is how the Great Depression occurred. None of these things happened overnight. The downward slide continued for many months after the stock market crash, as the nation's economy slowly collapsed.

At first, President Hoover's public outlook was confident. On October 25, the day after the crash began, he tried to reassure the American people. He told reporters, "The fundamental business of the country . . . is on a very sound and prosperous basis . . . which indicates a very healthy situation."[7] Many experts agreed. *The New York Times* reported that the crisis would be temporary.

Privately, however, the president was deeply concerned.[8] In late November he called business and labor union leaders to a series of meetings at the White House. The nation faced a long and serious economic depression, he told them, unless all would voluntarily cooperate to end the crisis. To help prevent such a depression, labor leaders agreed to withdraw demands for an increase in wages. Business groups promised not to lay off workers.

Hoover also turned to the state and federal governments for help. He requested that governors speed up work on planned public projects such as roads and state office buildings. The president asked Congress to cut taxes to ease the burden on the average taxpayer and to double the amount of spending on dams, harbors, and other federal government construction projects.

In part, these requests were designed to provide jobs for unemployed workers. Such government spending would also boost production by companies that supplied materials. Hoover hoped that government spending for materials and on workers' pay would give many people money to start buying things again.

For a while, Hoover's voluntary plan seemed to be working. "I am convinced we have now passed the worst," he reported in the spring of 1930. "With continued unity of effort we shall rapidly recover."[9] In June, however, a group of bankers and religious leaders warned that unemployment was spreading. Hoover told them they were wrong. In the end, however, it was the president who proved to be wrong.

8

BLAME IT ON HOOVER

As unemployment and other economic conditions worsened, President Hoover remained convinced that "the genius of modern business" could end the Depression.[1] He refused to listen to anyone who suggested otherwise. Allan Hoover, then enrolled at Harvard business school, presented his father with a technical analysis of the Depression. Hoover dismissed even his son's opinions as "bosh."[2]

What the president failed to recognize was that major changes had taken place in the nation's economy. By the late 1920s, the ability of industries to make goods had exceeded Americans' abilities to buy and use them. The very technology and business efficiency that Hoover had encouraged during his years as secretary of commerce was now the source of the troubles.

Hoping to help American businesses and save jobs, Congress passed a high protective tariff in the spring of 1930. A tariff is a tax placed on foreign goods produced overseas to be sold in the United States. The tax, or tariff, raises the price of those goods so that they cost more than similar items made in America. It is designed to protect American businesses by discouraging shoppers from buying foreign-made goods and encouraging them to buy items made in their own country. The 1930 tariff was proposed by the Smoot-Hawley bill, named after the legislators who brought it to Congress.

More than a thousand financial experts, 40 percent of the nation's Republican newspapers, and business leaders in both political parties urged Hoover to reject the tariff bill. Representatives of twenty-four other countries warned the president that the tariff would have terrible consequences.[3] Again Hoover insisted he knew best, and he signed the bill into law.

Once more, events proved the president wrong. By reducing sales of foreign-made goods in the United States, the Smoot-Hawley Tariff damaged the economies of other countries. Many were still struggling to recover financially from World War I. For example, Great Britain and France had borrowed huge sums of money from the United States in order to fight the war. As sales of their goods in America fell off, these countries could no longer afford to repay their loans.

In addition, the Smoot-Hawley Tariff actually hurt American business. To get revenge, other countries reacted to Hoover's action by putting high tariffs on American products. The result was that the overseas sales of American companies fell at the same time that sales were falling at home. Furthermore, by reducing international trade, the American tariff helped plunge the entire world into economic depression.

The results of the Smoot-Hawley Tariff also allowed Hoover to blame other countries for the worsening depression at home. It was the refusal of foreign countries to buy American products, he said, that was causing American workers to lose their jobs. He lashed out at foreign leaders as "cheap politicians" and "selfish men."[4] A reporter observed one of these attacks during an interview in the president's office. Hoover "burst out at me with a volley of angry words . . . against the politicians and foreign governments," the journalist recalled, "in language that he must have learned in a mining camp."[5]

However, despite the differences over trade, Hoover tried to work with foreign leaders on other world problems. Most important, the president hoped to gain Great Britain's support for a treaty to set limits on the size of the navies of the world's major powers. Similar treaties in the 1920s had failed to ease tensions as nations rearmed after World War I.

Hoover was especially concerned about Japan's rising power in the Pacific.[6] However, the London Naval Conference that Great Britain hosted in 1930 did little to solve this problem. The Japanese emerged from the conference bitter. The treaty that the conference adopted required their navy to be smaller than those of Great Britain and the United States.

By World War I, Japan had become the most powerful nation in Asia. Japanese officials looked overseas for sources of raw materials for Japan's growing industries and for new places to sell its products. One place where they tried to gain influence was Manchuria, a region of China that had rich deposits of coal and iron ore. As the world depression reached Japan, its military leaders claimed that expansion would cure their country's economic problems.

When Japanese troops seized Manchuria in 1931, Hoover's fears about Japan's intentions were realized. Secretary of State Henry L. Stimson favored cutting off trade with Japan as a punishment for its actions. However, Hoover believed that action might make the situation worse. The United States had no interests in China over which it was worth risking war with Japan, the president said privately. He called for a much more cautious response.[7]

In January 1933, the Hoover administration issued a statement of policy that soon became known as the Stimson Doctrine. It said that the United States would not recognize any nation's right to territory gained by force. However, without the willingness to use American military power to back it up, this doctrine was a feeble warning. The Japanese-American rivalry continued to build.

As Hoover tried to deal with growing international problems, conditions at home continued to worsen. However, he still clung to the approach to emergencies that had worked so well during the food crisis of World War I: public statements and voluntary cooperation. In fact, what was really needed was for the government to take charge and help plan the economy. However,

As Lou Hoover (right) looks on, President Hoover opens the 1930 baseball season by throwing out the first ball. The man with the mustache seated to the left of Hoover is Secretary of the Treasury Andrew Mellon.

Hoover rejected the idea of government control over the economy. He felt that government intervention was too close to the practice of communism. "Progress is born of cooperation in the community—not from governmental restraints," Hoover had stated in his inaugural address.[8] He continued to cling to that belief.

By the fall of 1930, about 4 million Americans were out of work. In the congressional elections that November, the Democrats blamed Hoover for the Depression. They took control of both houses of

Congress. A great political battle then developed. The Democrats wanted the president to do more, while Hoover insisted that his policy of nonintervention was the best one.

"Why is it," the president complained, "when a man is . . . doing the best he can, that certain men . . . seek to oppose everything he does, just to oppose him?"[9] Hoover longed for the days when he was the sole head of his operation. He resented having to deal with congressional leaders. "Those Democratic swine," he called them.[10] Hoover joked that if only he were allowed to be a dictator for six months, he could save the nation.[11]

Finally, in late 1931, Hoover gave in to outside pressures. He proposed that Congress create the Reconstruction Finance Corporation (RFC). This government agency made loans to businesses whose recovery was critical to the country's economy. It even loaned money to state and local governments. However, Hoover would not let the RFC make loans to individuals.

Nevertheless, the RFC was not enough. The Depression got even worse. In some states, one out of every four workers was without a job. Thousands of banks had closed. These bank failures deprived millions of depositors of what remained of their savings. Tens of thousands of Americans lost their homes. They lived in shacks that they fashioned from scraps of cardboard, lumber, metal, and whatever other materials they could find. Entire towns of such shacks sprang up. People bitterly called these towns "Hoovervilles." Comedian Will Rogers made the not-so-funny observation that in

Communist Russia there was no freedom, but at least everyone had a job.[12]

As food riots occurred in some cities, Hoover began to lose support among members of his own party. "For God's sake," cried one Republican senator, "get something done to feed the people who are hungry."[13] In rejecting these appeals for direct government aid, the president told reporters:

> I have indeed spent much of my life in fighting hardship and starvation. . . . I recall that in all the organizations with which I have been connected over these many years, the foundation [basic method] has been . . . self-help. . . . I am confident that our people have the resources . . . and kindness of spirit to meet this situation in the way they have met their problems over generations.[14]

Such public statements caused the newspapers to portray the president as insensitive to people's suffering. His reserved personality contributed to this image. When advisers urged Hoover to bypass the press and use radio to talk directly to the people, he declined. He admitted, "I only wish I could say what is in my heart."[15] Somehow, however, he felt unable to speak in such emotional terms.

On another occasion, hearing that some fellow engineers were having tough times, Hoover told a friend that he wanted to help them. "But I don't want anybody to get help if he doesn't need it," the president cautioned.[16] Hoover was talking about private assistance. But this statement also explains why his principles and his strict Quaker work ethic led him to oppose government aid programs.

An unemployed man (far left) tries to earn money during the Great Depression by selling apples on the street.

Hoover believed that government welfare would destroy people's drive to work hard and pursue success. To Hoover, these were the very qualities that made the nation great. Therefore, in July 1932, he vetoed a bill that would have given direct government aid to the unemployed. By that time, more than 12 million Americans were out of work. In addition, the Bonus Army was marching through the streets of Washington, D.C., chanting about the president and Secretary of the Treasury Andrew Mellon:

> Mellon pulled the whistle,
> Hoover rang the bell,
> Wall Street gave the signal,
> And the country went to Hell![17]

On the morning of July 29, 1932, New York governor Franklin Roosevelt studied the front page of *The New York Times*. There for the nation to see were pictures of the United States Army brutally attacking the Bonus Army in the nation's capital the night before. Roosevelt told an aide that the Democrats did not have to worry about Hoover any more.

However, reelection was not important enough to Hoover for him to forsake his principles. Although his enemies were concerned about the next election, Hoover maintained he was concerned about the next generation of Americans.

A grim-faced President Hoover (in top hat) leaves the Capitol after a stormy session with Congress over how best to deal with the effects of the Great Depression.

The Democratic party had begun to work for Hoover's defeat soon after he took office in 1929. The party hired Charles Michelson to be the first full-time publicity director in the history of American politics. It gave him a million-dollar budget with which to destroy Hoover's popularity. Michelson wrote anti-Hoover speeches for other Democrats. He also got stories placed in newspapers and on the radio that were intended to make Hoover look bad.

Trivial information about the White House began to appear in the news—for example, that Lou Hoover's driving "terrified" the wives of Cabinet members; that the president broke the speed limit when he drove to Camp Rapidan; even that the Hoovers' dog bit a Marine. Hoover tried to respond to such stories, but when he tried to stop the leaks to the press, the Democrats accused him of censorship.

Hoover's reaction to news reports that were untrue was often an angry one. For example, the Democrats blamed him for deaths in a food riot that never even took place. Another false report accused Hoover of making a fortune through secret food deals at a time when people were starving. Hoover ranted that there was a place reserved in Hell for people who spread such lies. His dramatic emotional reaction often caused these stories to receive even wider news coverage.

Michelson's tactics were highly successful. By the start of the 1932 campaign, they had helped turn most of the nation against the president. Millions of suffering Americans now blamed Hoover alone for the Depression. Will Rogers summed up the country's

SOURCE DOCUMENT

a -11/22/32 →

November 13, 1932

Pres. Herbert C. Hoover
Washington, D.C.
My Dear President:

THE WHITE HOUSE
NOV 14 1932
RECEIVED

For about half an hour on the morning of <u>November 23, 1932</u>. I am to be President Hoover. You see, Mr. President, out of our entire High school the faculty chose me to play that part in our Thanksgiving play because I am said to resemble you closely even though I am only thirteen years old. I deeply appreciate this honor but I feel that it would be swell if you could find time to write a few lines saying in them what you would say to a jobless father and family. stricken by the depression and trying make ends meet.

I am hopefully waiting for November 23rd because I feel certain that before that time I will receive a letter from the President of the United States.

Admiringly yours
Robert H. Davidson

President Hoover received many letters from children. In 1932, a teenage boy wrote to the president, asking what Hoover could say to Americans suffering from the effects of the Depression.

mood: If someone bit into an apple and found a worm in it, he joked, Hoover would get the blame.[18]

The reelection campaign was difficult for Hoover. When he arrived to give a speech in Detroit, an angry mob met him at the train station. In his home state of Iowa, some two thousand protesters shouted while he spoke. After a speech in Washington, D.C., almost no

SOURCE DOCUMENT

This editorial cartoon shows how many Americans felt about President Hoover by 1932, as the country approached the worst times of the Depression.

one applauded. The president trembled visibly when delivering some of these talks.[19]

In his speeches Hoover stuck to the issues. The Democrats then claimed the president was cold and uncaring. Only once during the campaign did Hoover drop his public reserve and respond to the Democrats' attacks. Finally, in October he lashed out:

> When you are told that the president of the United States, who by the most sacred trust of our nation is president of all the people, a man of your own blood and upbringing, has sat in the White House for the last three years of your misfortune without troubling to know your burdens, without heartaches over your miseries . . . then I say to you that such statements are deliberate, intolerable falsehoods.[20]

Hoover's public image as a cold and uncaring leader could not have been further from the truth. Secretly, he gave thousands of dollars of his own money to private charities, and quietly he raised thousands more. When he found out that children near Camp Rapidan had no school, he donated the money to build one and to hire a teacher. Yet Hoover never permitted his good deeds to become news. His Quaker beliefs had taught him that helping people should be a personal and private duty, not a cheap publicity stunt.

In November 1932, as everyone, including Hoover, expected, Franklin Delano Roosevelt won an easy victory. He polled 57 percent of the vote and defeated the president in forty-two of the forty-eight states. Just four years after being elected in one of the greatest landslides in history, Hoover had been turned out of office in a landslide of equal proportion.

On Inauguration Day, the custom is for the outgoing and incoming presidents to ride together to the ceremony. On March 4, 1933, the chill in the open car was more biting than the chill in the air. Several times, Roosevelt attempted to start a conversation, but Hoover was so angry that he barely replied. As soon as the inaugural ceremony was over, the Hoovers left Washington. During the twelve years that Roosevelt occupied the White House, Hoover never returned.

The former president was now fifty-eight years old. What he later came to call his "wilderness years" had begun.

9

THE WILDERNESS YEARS AND AFTER

"O n economic and political questions I am silent," Hoover told reporters on his return to Palo Alto, California, immediately after Roosevelt's inauguration. "Even on fishing I am silent."[1] For months the ex-president kept his word. Every morning he walked his dog on the Stanford University campus. He read about thirty newspapers each day and worked on books and articles that he planned to write.

Hoover also devoted time to a collection of research materials he had established at Stanford after World War I. In addition, he and Lou traveled, covering roughly eight thousand miles in ten weeks, visiting mines and trout streams, and calling on family and friends. The couple continued giving gifts to charities. They also gave money to poor children and unemployed people they met in their travels.

Yet Herbert Hoover did not find peace. Both his sons, Allan and Bert Jr., were accused of improper dealings with government agencies, and they both became targets of government investigations. Although his sons were eventually cleared of any wrongdoing, Hoover resented these and other continuing attacks by the Democrats.[2] Criticisms of his policies as president appeared almost daily in newspapers. So did personal smears. Once, a newspaper deliberately misreported Hoover's stop at a soft drink stand as a visit to a saloon. Hoover responded, "Would it not be decent public policy not to circulate lies intended to humiliate decent citizens—let alone an ex-president. . . ."[3]

Accompanied by their sons and grandchildren, former president and Mrs. Hoover leave their Palo Alto home to call on friends on Christmas Eve 1933.

Hoover became the target of other political slights. For example, the Democrats changed the name of Hoover Dam to Boulder Dam. Roosevelt did not invite him to the ceremony when the dam opened in 1935, even though Hoover had been responsible for the dam's construction. Roosevelt also denied Secret Service protection to Hoover after he left the White House. This was at a time when Hoover was probably the most hated man in America and had reason to fear for his life. He never forgave Roosevelt for this lack of respect.[4]

In late 1934, Hoover began to fight back. In books, articles, and speeches he attacked the "New Deal." This was the name of Roosevelt's series of programs and economic reforms to end the Depression. Hoover blasted the New Deal as big government interference that would deprive Americans of their rights and freedoms.

Some Republicans wanted Hoover to run for president again in 1936. However, party leaders opposed his candidacy. Hoover did not wish to divide the party, so he did not campaign for the nomination. Instead it went to Alfred Landon, the governor of Kansas. Hoover never again held elected office.

However, Hoover's return to public life made him once again the most important Republican of the era. He continued to be one of Roosevelt's most outspoken critics until the president's death in 1945. By 1937, Hoover had organized anti-Roosevelt groups in about twenty states and was regularly speaking out against the president on national radio.

By the mid-1930s, dictators had seized control of Italy and Germany, and military officers gained control over the government of Japan. These foreign leaders began to talk of making their nations great by conquering other peoples and creating empires. In 1935, Italy took action on its threat by invading the African nation of Ethiopia. Two years later Japan expanded out of Manchuria to attack the rest of China.

As countries again drifted toward world war, Hoover used the valuable contacts he had made during his globe-trotting years to try and prevent it. In 1938, he revisited Europe, the scene of his triumphs during World War I. While he was in Germany, its dictator, Adolf Hitler, requested a meeting. Hoping to improve German-American relations, Hoover accepted Hitler's invitation. Later, he reported that during their hour-long talk Hitler had flown into several uncontrollable rages. The German leader was intelligent, but dangerous and "insane," Hoover said. He returned to America convinced that Hitler would soon go to war.[5] He was also convinced that the United States should stay out of it.

With a Quaker's distaste for violence, the former president tried to remind Americans of the horrors of World War I: "Like ants, they advanced under the thunder and belching volcanoes of 10,000 guns," Hoover wrote in 1939 of a World War I battle that had involved a million and a half men. "Their lives were thrown away until half a million had died. . . . That is war. Let us not forget."[6]

World War II began in late 1939, when Germany attacked its neighbor, Poland. At first, the United States stayed out of the war, but Hoover still attacked Roosevelt's policies. Despite America's supposed neutrality, Roosevelt openly supported Great Britain and France against Germany and Italy, and Hoover feared that such favoritism would eventually drag America into the war.

At the same time, however, Hoover went on radio to condemn strongly Hitler's persecution of Germany's Jews. He also helped organize and raise funds for a private effort to rescue German Jews before it was too late, and they were exterminated by Hitler's Nazi troops. In 1940, Hoover proposed that a new nation be established in Africa as a refuge for Jews fleeing Europe.[7]

In 1940, Hoover tried once more for the Republican presidential nomination; however, it went to Indiana businessman Wendell L. Willkie. Although by this time, many Americans were agreeing with Hoover's attacks on Roosevelt's New Deal, Republican party leaders still did not want Hoover to run again. This was because the public still blamed him for what the Democrats called the "Hoover Depression."

The nation had not yet recovered from the Depression by 1940. One incident sums up how many Americans still felt about their former leader. In 1939, Hoover dedicated a memorial in Charleston, West Virginia. During the ceremony the former president was honored with a twenty-one-gun salute. After the guns were fired, a man in the audience shaded his eyes and peered over to where Hoover was standing. "By gum," he said, "they missed him."[8] Despite his unpopularity, Hoover continued to be a powerful Republican voice against Roosevelt. However, he had to speak out on his own, without any official party support.

In 1941, as Japanese armies advanced across Asia, American relations with Japan worsened. While leaders of both nations discussed their differences, Hoover worked behind the scenes as a private citizen. Again, he tried to use his world contacts to prevent war. These peace-seeking efforts broke down just before Japan attacked the American fleet at Pearl Harbor, in Hawaii, on December 7, 1941.

Despite his belief that Roosevelt's policies had led the nation into war, Hoover called on Americans to unite behind the president. However, privately he pledged, "There is not the remotest possibility that I will have anything to do with the conduct of this war."[9]

This was one subject on which Hoover and Roosevelt agreed. Some prominent Americans recommended that Hoover help organize the nation's war effort, as he had done during World War I. However, the president rejected the idea. He did not want to risk improving Hoover's poor public image. "I'm not going to raise him from the dead," Roosevelt admitted.[10]

Hoover devoted most of his time during the war to his writing. Writing was not an easy task for the man who had barely mastered English composition in college. Nevertheless, in two books, Hoover presented his views on how to keep peace in the world. He also wrote his three-volume life story, *The Memoirs of Herbert Hoover*, during this period.

World War II was also a time of personal tragedy for Hoover. In 1934 he and Lou had moved into an apartment at the Waldorf-Astoria, a luxury hotel in New York City. It was in this apartment that on January 7, 1944,

Lou Hoover died unexpectedly of a heart attack at the age of sixty-eight.

In settling Lou's affairs, Hoover found checks made out to her for thousands of dollars that Lou had never cashed. The checks were repayments for loans she had made to needy people. Not cashing these checks had been Lou's way of turning these loans into gifts. Lou's will included a letter to Allan and Bert Jr.: "You have been lucky boys to have had such a father," she wrote. "And I am a lucky woman to have had my life's trail alongside the path of three such men and boys."[11]

In April 1945 President Roosevelt also died. The passing of his old enemy seemed to provide a sort of personal release for Hoover. Roosevelt's death also allowed him to return to government service. In early 1946, the new president, Harry S. Truman, another Democrat, asked Hoover to head a program to feed Europe after the devastation of World War II.

With four of his helpers from the World War I relief effort, the seventy-two-year-old ex-president began a trip to Europe, the Middle East, and Asia. He covered thirty-five thousand miles in fifty-seven days. During this time he visited twenty-two countries and gathered information on conditions in about a dozen more.

Never before in setting up relief programs was so much work done in so short a time. Hoover convinced leaders in nations with enough food to cut back and provide the surplus to needy nations. Within months, his efforts had saved several hundred million people from starvation.

In May 1946, Hoover was off again on a similar tour

of Latin America. His trips made many Americans aware of world hunger for the first time.[12] His actions also increased public support for the Marshall Plan.[13] This was the economic and political program that Truman launched to rebuild Europe after the war.

In 1947 the Republicans gained control of Congress for the first time since the Depression, and Truman accepted the majority party's proposal that Boulder Dam's name be changed back to its original Hoover Dam. The president also asked Hoover to head a study to reorganize the government. Roosevelt's New Deal and World War II had made the government big and expensive to operate.[14] To Hoover, the idea of making it smaller and more efficient was a long-held dream.[15]

Hoover and a staff of about three hundred experts worked for two years on the study. In 1949, the Hoover Commission issued a long report that proposed 273 changes in the government. Congress eventually adopted about 70 percent of Hoover's recommendations, which ultimately saved the taxpayers several billion dollars.[16]

A similar study of the government's social and economic policies was ordered by President Dwight D. Eisenhower in 1953. Again, Hoover was asked to head the effort. However, Eisenhower rejected many ideas of this second Hoover Commission as old-fashioned and extreme. Only about a third of its suggestions actually became law. This public denial disappointed Hoover.[17]

After the publication of the second (Eisenhower) Hoover Commission's report in May 1955, Herbert Hoover retired from public service. His brother, Tad, had

President Harry S. Truman (right) chats with Herbert Hoover in 1947, after naming Hoover head of a commission to make the government more efficient.

died earlier that year. Now Hoover wanted to devote the time he had left to activities and causes he held dear. These included his writing, Stanford University, and the Boys Clubs of America.

In 1958, Hoover published a biography of Woodrow Wilson, his old boss during the World War I relief days. He was the first former president to write the story of another. The book became an instant best-seller. Later, Hoover also completed a four-volume history of world hunger, which he had started during World War II, and he published a short book on his hobby of fishing.

However, at eighty-nine years old, Hoover was too

old to wade in his beloved icy trout streams. Now, he preferred ocean fishing in the balmy Florida Keys. He spent several weeks there each winter. Much of his summer was passed in California. Sometimes Harry Truman joined him in these vacation spots.

Wherever Hoover went, he always took projects with him. Asked by a reporter for the secret to his long and vigorous life, Hoover offered a simple reply: "Work."[18] However, as his health began to fail, he complained that he was only able to work eight to ten hours a day.[19]

A typical day for the elderly former president was still busy. His Waldorf-Astoria suite included offices, and he employed a staff of eight clerks and secretaries who scheduled his appointments, opened his mail, and did his typing. Mealtimes were Hoover's visiting hours, and he frequently had guests at breakfast, lunch, and dinner. At the end of each day, his secretaries left him a stack of letters to be answered that evening.

Herbert Hoover (right) fishes for trout in Oregon's McKenzie River in 1955. Hoover never lost his boyhood love of fishing.

Hoover devoted his early evenings to reading or playing cards with friends. Then he answered his mail, sometimes staying up until 2:00 A.M. to finish the job. He particularly liked mail from children, and he replied to thousands of their letters each year. In 1962, he published some of his favorite children's letters and his answers to them in a book entitled *On Growing Up*.

Despite his advancing years, Hoover still made about six speeches and other public appearances a year. In 1958, he officially represented the United States at the world's fair in Brussels, Belgium. There he discovered that nearly all his friends from the old CRB days were dead. In 1960, he referred to his own impending death in a speech to the Republican National Convention. He warned the delegates that they would probably not see him again. "Unless some miracle comes to me from the Good Lord, this is finally it," Hoover said.[20] Near his eighty-sixth birthday, he restated to the convention his faith in the nation he had served for so long:

> I have lived a long life. I have witnessed, and even taken part in, many great and threatening crises. With each time they have been surmounted [overcome], the American Dream has become more real. . . . If the American people are guided aright, there will be no decline and fall in American civilization.[21]

In 1962, Hoover turned eighty-eight at his birthplace, West Branch, Iowa. The occasion was marked by the dedication of the Hoover Presidential Library. It now houses his official papers and mementos of his half century of public service. With the Depression now a distant memory in most people's minds, a crowd of forty-five thousand flooded the little town to honor one of America's greatest citizens. At least half of them had not even been born when he was president. Hoover was feeble and had to sit in a chair as he delivered his speech. On his return to New York he was hospitalized. Doctors diagnosed him with colon cancer.

By June 1963, the former president was confined to a wheelchair. Nevertheless, he continued to work five to six hours a day on letters and books that he was writing. By this time, he rarely left his apartment, depending instead on visitors and newspapers for information about the world outside. Still, when President John F. Kennedy was assassinated that November, the ailing Hoover tried to respond to one more crisis. "I am ready to serve our government in any capacity," he wrote to the new president, Lyndon B. Johnson.[22] However, Hoover's desire to help was greater than his capacity to do so. Two nurses had been added to his staff, which increasingly became like a family.

In 1964, as Hoover's health continued to decline, major figures in American politics came to his apartment to pay their respects. Richard Nixon, President Johnson, and Supreme Court Chief Justice Earl Warren were among his visitors. Hoover warmly welcomed such visits. "I sit here most of the day with these nurses and we don't speak the same language," he confided to one visitor. "They're really wonderful for me and do everything they can, but that isn't my type of talk."[23] On August 10, 1964, his ninetieth birthday, sixteen states declared it "Herbert Hoover Day."

One of Hoover's last acts was to send a telegram to

former president Harry Truman. In it he wished his old friend a speedy recovery from injuries Truman had suffered when he slipped in the bathtub. Two days later, on October 16, Hoover began to bleed internally in his stomach and intestines. He refused to go to the hospital. Too old and weak for surgery, Herbert Hoover died at home on October 20, 1964. Sons Allan and Bert Jr. were by his side at the end.

SOURCE DOCUMENT

HARRY S. TRUMAN
INDEPENDENCE, MISSOURI

June 10, 1963

Dear Mr. President:

I am sorry to have been so long in acknowledging your good wishes but I didn't receive a single birthday telegram that I appreciated more than I did yours.

I know you have the same experience, however, and we understand each other.

Sincerely yours,

Harry Truman sent this note thanking Hoover for remembering his seventy-ninth birthday. Their long friendship was unusual for two former presidents of opposing political parties.

10
LEGACY

O n October 25, 1964, Herbert Hoover was buried in West Branch, Iowa. His final resting place is on a grassy knoll in sight of both his presidential library and the cottage where he was born. It was a simple service. There were no speeches to praise the man who perhaps did more for world hunger than anyone else in America. Although at one time he was called the most hated person in America, seventy-five thousand people were present at the gravesite. This sign of respect shows the effects of time on Hoover's reputation. The public's opinion of the man has continued to improve since his death.

Today, we know that Hoover did not personally cause the Depression. That dark period in American history resulted from years of world and national events and policies that were beyond his control. We also know now that there was probably little he could have done to make the Depression less severe. Historians now believe that Roosevelt's New Deal did not magically improve the severe economic problems. The Depression lasted until the United States entered World War II, eight years after Roosevelt took office. The facts suggest that government-aid programs would not have worked for Hoover, either.

Late in life Hoover joked that a more favorable image of his strength and deeds had emerged primarily because he had outlived his enemies.[1] This analysis is only partly true. Indeed, Herbert Hoover lived longer after leaving office than any other president, but at the time of his death his respected status was due to much more than a long life. Hoover made good use of his years in retirement. He left a legacy that continues to touch American lives in many ways.

During his long life, Hoover visited nearly every country on the globe. He lived in London, New York City, Washington, D.C., and San Francisco. Yet he never lost his Quaker values or those of small-town America. These include his dedication to service, his belief in inner strength and individual freedom, and his conviction that people should always help each other.

Hoover's values and the difficulties of his childhood as an orphan inspired his lifelong dedication to young people. His relief efforts on behalf of children continued long after World War I. After World War II, he helped found two of the major relief organizations still operating in the world today: the United Nations

Children's Fund (UNICEF) and Cooperative Assistance in Relief Everywhere (CARE).[2]

To help children in America, in 1928 Hoover convinced President Coolidge to proclaim a national Child Health Day, still celebrated in October every year. In addition, as president, Hoover called for a White House conference on children. Its report served for years as a handbook for social workers across the country.

"If we could have but one generation of properly born, trained, educated and healthy children, a thousand other problems of government would vanish," Hoover once said.[3]

For most of his life, he was involved with groups that sought such goals. He made large gifts and raised funds for both the Boy Scouts and the Girl Scouts. Lou Hoover served as president of the Girl Scouts.

In 1936, Herbert Hoover was asked to head the Boys Clubs of America. This organization provides leisure activities and other benefits for children. He served in the position for nearly thirty years. Hoover built up the network of Boys Clubs from 140 to more than six hundred organizations in approximately four hundred cities. He tried to attend the opening of every new club. In all, he helped offer an alternative to gangs and the streets to a half-million boys. Today the organization is called the Boys and Girls Clubs of America.

One of Hoover's first acts as chairman of the Boys Clubs was to remove the phrase "for white boys only" from its constitution. In both his private and public duties, Hoover was ahead of his time on civil rights issues. In 1928, he ended racial segregation in the

Eighty-seven-year-old Herbert Hoover cuts a cake in 1961, celebrating his twenty-fifth anniversary as head of the Boys Clubs of America.

Commerce Department by ordering black and white employees to work in the same offices. This action came roughly twenty years before race discrimination officially ended throughout the federal government.[4]

As president, Hoover continued these fair hiring policies. He ordered an end to race discrimination in hiring on the Hoover Dam project. In 1932, he also became the first president to ban sex discrimination in government jobs.[5]

Hoover's other "firsts" are also notable. He was the first of only two Quaker presidents. (Richard Nixon is the other.) He was also the first president to be born west of the Mississippi River, as well as the first president to be elected from a western state; his legal residence at the time was California.

Many of Hoover's actions, both in and out of office, continue to be important. His practice of licensing the airwaves as secretary of commerce is continued by the Federal Communications Commission (FCC). This practice allows each station to broadcast programs clearly without mixing in the signals of other stations. Hoover's regulation of the aviation industry anticipated the work of today's Federal Aviation Agency (FAA). An agreement about the Colorado River that Hoover negotiated with seven western states in the 1920s still remains the basis for water use in those states.

Stanford University benefited in many ways from its long association with Hoover. He served for forty-nine years on its board of trustees. During that time he gave hundreds of thousands of dollars to the college and raised millions more. After Lou's death, Hoover donated their California house to Stanford. Today it is called the Lou Henry Hoover House and serves as the official residence for every Stanford president.

The most visible legacy of Herbert Hoover on the Stanford campus is the Hoover Tower, a prominent landmark. You can see it from the air on the approach to San Francisco International Airport. The 285-foot tower is the home of the Hoover Institution on War, Revolution, and Peace. Hoover founded it as a library after World War I. He recognized the need to protect vital records from the ravages of war. Today the institute is one of the world's greatest "think tanks," or research institutes on economic, political, and social change.

Hoover was also responsible for changes in government that created a stronger and more efficient executive branch. The president's role today as overall manager of the government is largely the result of the first Hoover Commission's efforts.[6]

Ironically, Hoover was also partly responsible for the policies of the New Deal. Many of its programs stemmed from Hoover's ideas when he was president. For example, Hoover's plan for old-age pensions formed the basis for Social Security. Likewise, Roosevelt's famous Good Neighbor policy toward Latin America grew out of the pledge of help that Hoover made during his 1928 Latin American tour.

In 1974, Rexford Tugwell, a key Roosevelt adviser in the 1930s, finally acknowledged the nation's debt to the man the Democrats so harshly criticized during his presidency and after. "We didn't admit it at the time," Tugwell revealed, "but practically the whole New Deal was extrapolated [developed] from programs that Hoover started."[7]

One of the greatest testimonials of all is that in fifty years of public service, Hoover accepted no pay for any of his activities, either in his private duties or his government positions. He even served as president of the United States for free. Although the Constitution required that he receive a salary, Hoover donated all of it to charity. "Why should I take pay for what I have done," he once said. "I was a boy with nothing and this magnificent country of ours gave me my education and my opportunity."[8]

It is not likely that Herbert Hoover will ever be ranked among the nation's top presidents. The scars of the Great Depression have almost certainly eliminated that possibility. Five different polls of historians all ranked Hoover as an "average" president.[9] Americans who felt the effects of the Depression firsthand would probably not even rank him that high.

Hoover was full of strength and greatness, but he also displayed many contradictions and weaknesses. He was brilliant and had great vision for the future. Yet he was stubborn and refused to accept any ideas he did not understand. He fed millions of the world's people during the world wars and after. Yet he would not compromise his principles while Americans starved during the Depression. He led huge organizations but preferred to work alone.

Hoover was a world figure. However, he was also painfully withdrawn and shy. In later years, he finally admitted that he was terrified every time he gave a speech.[10] His personal contradictions and steady insistence on privacy make him a difficult man to evaluate. Even some longtime friends claimed that they never really knew him. One acquaintance compared Hoover's personality to a fortress with all the gates closed. There was nothing to see, he said, "but a stretch of blank wall."[11]

Therefore, we must judge the man by his deeds. "When all is said and done," Hoover once wrote, "accomplishment is all that counts."[12] Although his record as president is tarnished by the Great Depression, his overall service to the nation, the world, and its children makes him one of America's outstanding citizens.

Hoover Tower on the Stanford University campus is a library, a research institute, and Hoover's most visible legacy.

Chronology

1874—Born in West Branch, Iowa, on August 10.

1880—Father dies of typhoid fever at age thirty-four on December 10.

1884—Mother dies of pneumonia at age thirty-four on February 24.

1885—Sent to live at the home of uncle John Minthorn in Newberg, Oregon.

1888—Moves with uncle's family to Salem, Oregon; employed in business started by his uncle.

1891—Enrolls at Stanford University in Palo Alto, California.

1895—Graduates from Stanford with geology degree; employed as miner in Nevada City, California.

1896—Employed by mining engineer Louis Janin of San Francisco; works on assignments for employer in California, Colorado, and New Mexico.

1897—Employed by Bewick, Moreing & Company of London, England; sent to Australia for two years.

1899—Marries Lou Henry in Monterey, California, on February 10; sent by employer to China for three years.

1903—First child, Herbert Clark (Bert) Jr., born in London on August 4.

1907—Second son, Allan Henry, born in London on July 17.

1908—Resigns from Bewick, Moreing & Company; returns to United States to found own company.

1914—Directs European relief program during World War I and after.

1917—Appointed U.S. Food Administrator by President Woodrow Wilson; holds position for two years.

1921—Named secretary of commerce by President Warren Harding; serves for eight years under Harding and President Calvin Coolidge.

1928—Elected thirty-first president of United States; takes office in March 1929.

1929—Policies harshly criticized after stock market crashes on Black Tuesday, October 29, leading to the Great Depression.

1932—Orders United States Army to disperse the Bonus Army in Washington, D.C.; defeated for reelection by Franklin D. Roosevelt.

1933—Leaves office in March; returns to Palo Alto, California.

1934—Moves to New York City apartment in the Waldorf-Astoria Hotel.

1936—Unsuccessful in gaining Republican party nomination to run for president.

1940—Again unsuccessful in gaining Republican party nomination to run for president.

1944—Lou Henry Hoover dies in New York City on January 7.

1946—Appointed by President Harry S. Truman to head relief effort in Europe after World War II.

1947—Appointed by Truman to head Hoover Commission to reorganize government.

1953—Appointed by President Dwight D. Eisenhower to head second Hoover Commission to reorganize government.

1962—Herbert Hoover Presidential Library opens in West Branch, Iowa.

1964—Dies on October 20 in New York City.

Chapter Notes

Chapter 1. The Bonus Army

1. Martin L. Fausold, *The Presidency of Herbert C. Hoover* (Lawrence: University of Kansas Press, 1985), pp. 201–202.

2. David Burner, *Herbert Hoover: A Public Life* (New York: Alfred A. Knopf, 1979), pp. 308–309.

3. Gene Smith, *The Shattered Dream: Herbert Hoover and the Great Depression* (New York: William Morrow & Co., 1970), p. 140.

4. Herbert Hoover, *The Memoirs of Herbert Hoover*, vol. 3 (New York: The Macmillan Company, 1952), p. 226.

5. Edgar Robinson and Vaughn Bornet, *Herbert Hoover: President of the United States* (Stanford, Calif.: Hoover Institution Press, 1975), p. 234.

6. G. Smith, p. 160.

7. Frederick Lewis Allen, *Since Yesterday* (New York: Bantam Books, 1965), pp. 67–68.

8. Burner, p. 311.

9. *Public Papers of the Presidents of the United States: Herbert Hoover*, vol. 1 (Washington, D.C.: United States Government Printing Office, 1974), p. 340.

10. Ibid., p. 348.

11. Burner, p. 311.

12. Ibid., p. 312.

Chapter 2. The Orphan from Iowa

1. George H. Nash, *The Life of Herbert Hoover: The Engineer, 1874–1914* (New York: W. W. Norton & Co., 1983), pp. 3, 5.

2. Ibid., p. 4.

3. Ibid., p. 8; Herbert Hoover, *The Memoirs of Herbert Hoover*, vol. 1 (New York: The Macmillan Company, 1952), p. 7.

4. Nash, pp. 8–9; Eugene Lyons, *Herbert Hoover: A Biography* (Garden City, N.Y.: Doubleday & Company, Inc., 1964), p. 12.

5. Nash, p. 11.

6. David Burner, *Herbert Hoover: A Public Life* (New York: Alfred A. Knopf, 1979), p. 14.

7. Hoover, vol. 1, p. 11.

8. Nash, p. 17.

9. Burner, p. 14.

10. Nash, pp. 17–19.

11. Ibid., p. 21.

12. Richard Norton Smith, *An Uncommon Man: The Triumph of Herbert Hoover* (New York: Simon & Schuster, 1984), p. 67.

13. Nash, p. 23; Hoover, vol. 1, pp. 13–14.

14. Burner, p. 16.

15. Hoover, vol. 1, p. 15.

Chapter 3. Stanford Pioneer

1. Eugene Lyons, *Herbert Hoover: A Biography* (Garden City, N.Y.: Doubleday & Company, Inc., 1964), p. 25.

2. Dorothy Horton McGee, *Herbert Hoover: Engineer, Humanitarian, Statesman* (New York: Dodd, Mead & Co., 1966), p. 17.

3. Richard Norton Smith, *An Uncommon Man: The Triumph of Herbert Hoover* (New York: Simon & Schuster, 1984), p. 69.

4. George H. Nash, *The Life of Herbert Hoover: The Engineer, 1874–1914* (New York: W. W. Norton & Co., 1983), p. 30.

5. Herbert Hoover, *The Memoirs of Herbert Hoover*, vol. 1 (New York: The Macmillan Company, 1952), p. 18.

6. Nash, pp. 43–44.

7. Ibid., p. 49.

8. Ibid., p. 31.

9. Lyons, p. 25.

10. Nash, p. 36.

11. Ibid., p. 40.

12. Hoover, vol. 1, p. 23.

13. R. Smith, p. 71.

14. Lyons, p. 37.

15. Hoover, vol. 1, p. 26.

16. Nash, pp. 45–46; David Burner, *Herbert Hoover: A Public Life* (New York: Alfred A. Knopf, 1979), p. 23.

Chapter 4. The Globetrotter

1. George H. Nash, *The Life of Herbert Hoover: The Engineer, 1874–1914* (New York: W. W. Norton & Co., 1983), p. 53.

2. Richard Norton Smith, *An Uncommon Man: The Triumph of Herbert Hoover* (New York: Simon & Schuster, 1984), p. 74.

3. Nash, p. 62.

4. Eugene Lyons, *Herbert Hoover: A Biography* (Garden City, N.Y.: Doubleday & Company, Inc., 1964), p. 47.

5. Nash, p. 120.

6. Herbert Hoover, *The Memoirs of Herbert Hoover,* vol. 1, (New York: The Macmillan Company, 1952), p. 50.

7. David Burner, *Herbert Hoover: A Public Life* (New York: Alfred A. Knopf, 1979), p. 37.

8. Ibid., p. 38; Hoover, vol. 1, pp. 54–55.

9. Lyons, pp. 54–55.

10. Ibid., p. 66.

11. Nash, pp. 416, 509.

12. Wilton Eckley, *Herbert Hoover* (Boston: Twayne Publishers, 1980), p. 26.

13. R. Smith, p. 77.

14. Nash, p. 513.

15. Burner, p. 46.

16. Nash, p. 520.

17. Ibid., p. 510.

Chapter 5. Food Regulator of the World

1. Eugene Lyons, *Herbert Hoover: A Biography* (Garden City, N.Y.: Doubleday & Company, Inc., 1964), p. 75.

2. George H. Nash, *The Life of Herbert Hoover: The Humanitarian, 1914–1917* (New York: W. W. Norton & Co., 1983), pp. 10–11.

3. Lyons, p. 79; Richard Norton Smith, *An Uncommon Man: The Triumph of Herbert Hoover* (New York: Simon & Schuster, 1984), p. 81.

4. Lyons, pp. 81–82.

5. Dorothy Horton McGee, *Herbert Hoover: Engineer, Humanitarian, Statesman* (New York: Dodd, Mead & Co., 1966), p. 137.

6. Lyons, p. 101; David Burner, *Herbert Hoover: A Public Life* (New York: Alfred A. Knopf, 1979), p. 97.

7. McGee, p. 141.

8. Burner, p. 119.

9. Lyons, p. 118.

10. McGee, p. 162.

11. Ibid., p. 182.

Chapter 6. The Wonder Boy

1. Herbert Hoover, *The Memoirs of Herbert Hoover*, vol. 2 (New York: The Macmillan Company, 1952), p. 2.

2. Ibid., p. 5.

3. Joan Hoff Wilson, *Herbert Hoover: Forgotten Progressive* (Prospect Heights, Ill.: Waveland Press, 1975), p. 51.

4. Hoover, vol. 2, p. 5.

5. Dorothy Horton McGee, *Herbert Hoover: Engineer, Humanitarian, Statesman* (New York: Dodd, Mead & Co., 1966), p. 185.

6. Eugene Lyons, *Herbert Hoover: A Biography* (Garden City, N.Y.: Doubleday & Company, Inc., 1964), p. 160.

7. Richard Norton Smith et al., *Herbert Hoover Library and Museum: A Guide to the Exhibit Galleries* (West Branch, Iowa: Herbert Hoover Library and Museum, 1993), p. 32.

8. Lyons, p. 160.

9. R. Smith, p. 42

10. Hoover, vol. 2, p. 195.

11. Ibid., p. 207.

12. *The American Heritage Pictorial History of the Presidents of the United States*, vol. 2 (n.p.: American Heritage Publishing Co., 1968), p. 776.

13. Richard Norton Smith, *An Uncommon Man: The Triumph of Herbert Hoover* (New York: Simon & Schuster, 1984), p. 103.

Chapter 7. Good Times and Bad

1. *Public Papers of the Presidents of the United States: Herbert Hoover*, vol. 1 (Washington, D.C.: United States Government Printing Office, 1974), p. 11.

2. Martin L. Fausold, *The Presidency of Herbert C. Hoover* (Lawrence: University of Kansas Press, 1985), pp. 49–50.

3. Richard Norton Smith, *An Uncommon Man: The Triumph of Herbert Hoover* (New York: Simon & Schuster, 1984), p. 92.

4. David Burner, *Herbert Hoover: A Public Life* (New York: Alfred A. Knopf, 1979), p. 257.

5. Ibid.

6. R. Smith, p. 114.

7. *Public Papers*, vol. 1, p. 355.

8. R. Smith, p. 116.

9. Dorothy Horton McGee, *Herbert Hoover: Engineer, Humanitarian, Statesman* (New York: Dodd, Mead & Co., 1966), p. 229.

Chapter 8. Blame It on Hoover

1. Richard Norton Smith, *An Uncommon Man: The Triumph of Herbert Hoover* (New York: Simon & Schuster, 1984), p. 119.

2. Ibid., p. 121.

3. Joan Hoff Wilson, *Herbert Hoover: Forgotten Progressive* (Prospect Heights, Ill.: Waveland Press, 1975), p. 179.

4. Ibid., p. 163.

5. Ibid., pp. 162–163.

6. David Burner, *Herbert Hoover: A Public Life* (New York: Alfred A. Knopf, 1979), p. 290.

7. Ibid., pp. 294–296.

8. *Public Papers of the Presidents of the United States: Herbert Hoover*, vol. 1 (Washington, D.C.: United States Government Printing Office, 1974), p. 5.

9. R. Smith, p. 123.

10. Ibid., p. 121.

11. Ibid., p. 123.

12. Ibid., p. 125.

13. Ibid.

14. *Public Papers*, vol. 3, pp. 52–53.

15. R. Smith, p. 121.

16. Ibid., p. 120.

17. *The American Heritage Pictorial History of the Presidents of the United States*, vol. 2 (n.p.: American Heritage Publishing Co., 1968), p. 772.

18. R. Smith, p. 120.

19. Burner, pp. 314–315.

20. *Public Papers*, vol. 4, p. 326.

Chapter 9. The Wilderness Years and After

1. Richard Norton Smith, *An Uncommon Man: The Triumph of Herbert Hoover* (New York: Simon & Schuster, 1984), p. 172.

2. Eugene Lyons, *Herbert Hoover: A Biography* (Garden City, N.Y.: Doubleday & Company, Inc., 1964), p. 332.

3. R. Smith, p. 175.

4. Ibid., p. 164.

5. Ibid., p. 254.

6. Ibid., p. 266.

7. Arnold S. Rice, ed., *Herbert Hoover, 1874–1964: Chronology-Documents-Bibliographical Aids* (Dobbs Ferry, N.Y.: Oceana Publications, Inc., 1971), p. 31.

8. David Burner, *Herbert Hoover: A Public Life* (New York: Alfred A. Knopf, 1979), p. 332.

9. R. Smith, p. 307.

10. Ibid., p. 309.

11. Lyons, p. 373.

12. Ibid., pp. 389–390.

13. Burner, p. 335.

14. R. Smith, pp. 374–375.

15. Burner, p. 336.

16. Ibid., p. 337; R. Smith, p. 375.

17. Burner, p. 337; R. Smith, p. 409.

18. Ben Hibbs, "Happy Birthday Herbert Hoover," *Saturday Evening Post*, July 28, 1962, p. 66.

19. Lyons, p. 419; Gary Dean Best, *Herbert Hoover: The Postpresidential Years, 1933–1964*, vol. 2 (Stanford, Calif.: Hoover Institution Press, 1983), pp. 412–413.

20. Best, vol. 2, p. 415.

21. Lyons, p. 423.

22. R. Smith, p. 426.

23. Ibid., p. 428.

Chapter 10. Legacy

1. Richard Norton Smith, *An Uncommon Man: The Triumph of Herbert Hoover* (New York: Simon & Schuster, 1984), p. 15.

2. Ibid., p. 362.

3. Eugene Lyons, *Herbert Hoover: A Biography* (Garden City, N.Y.: Doubleday & Company, Inc., 1964), p. 327.

4. David Burner, *Herbert Hoover: A Public Life* (New York: Alfred A. Knopf, 1979), pp. 253, 256; Jeffrey Morris and Richard B. Morris, eds., *Encyclopedia of American History*, 7th ed. (New York: HarperCollins, 1996), pp. 498–499.

5. Burner, pp. 217, 223.

6. Ibid., p. 337; *CQ's Encyclopedia of American Government*, vol. 2 (Washington, D.C.: Congressional Quarterly Inc., 1994), p. 222.

7. Burner, p. 244.

8. Ben Hibbs, "Happy Birthday Herbert Hoover," *Saturday Evening Post*, July 28, 1962, p. 67.

9. Robert K. Murray and Tim H. Blessing, "The Presidential Performance Study: A Progress Report," *The Journal of American History*, December 1983, pp. 540–541.

10. Burner, p. 341.

11. Ibid., p. 339.

12. Joan Hoff Wilson, *Herbert Hoover: Forgotten Progressive* (Prospect Heights, Ill.: Waveland Press, 1975), p. 282.

Further Reading

Clinton, Susan. *Herbert Hoover*. Chicago: Children's Press, 1988.

Emery, Anne. *American Friend: Herbert Hoover*. Chicago: Rand McNally, 1967.

Fremon, David, K. *The Great Depression in American History*. Springfield, N.J.: Enslow Publishers, Inc., 1997.

Hilton, Suzanne. *The World of Young Herbert Hoover*. New York: Walker and Co., 1987.

Hoover, Herbert. *The Memoirs of Herbert Hoover*. 3 vols. New York: The Macmillan Company, 1952.

——————. *On Growing Up: Letters to American Boys & Girls*. New York: William Morrow & Company, 1962.

Kent, Zachary, *World War I: "The War to End Wars."* Springfield, N.J.: Enslow Publishers, Inc., 1994.

McGee, Dorothy Horton. *Herbert Hoover: Engineer, Humanitarian, Statesman*. New York: Dodd, Mead & Co., 1966.

Morris, Jeffrey. *The FDR Way*. New York: Scholastic, Inc., 1996.

Pietrusza, David, *The Roaring Twenties*. San Diego, Calif.: Lucent Books, 1997.

Spies, Karen Bornemann. *Franklin D. Roosevelt*. Springfield, N.J.: Enslow Publishers, Inc., 1999.

Trueblood, D. Elton. *The People Called Quakers*. Richmond, Ind.: Friends United, 1971.

Wilson, Carol Green. *Herbert Hoover, A Challenge for Today*. New York: The Evans Publishing Co., 1968.

Places to Visit

California

Stanford University. Palo Alto. (650) 725-3335. The home of Lou and Herbert Hoover. Exhibits at the Hoover Institution will give you an overview of their lives and careers. Open year-round.

Iowa

Herbert Hoover Library and Museum. West Branch. (319) 643-5301. Six museum galleries use photos, videos, and objects to detail each period of Hoover's life. A highlight is the re-created living room of his elegant Waldorf Astoria apartment. The graves of Lou and Herbert Hoover are a short walk from the museum. Open year-round.

Herbert Hoover National Historic Site. West Branch. (319) 643-2541. The site preserves the neighborhood where Hoover lived as a child. Buildings include the cottage where he was born, the Quaker meetinghouse, his school, and a replica of his father's blacksmith shop. Open year-round.

Nevada

Hoover Dam. Boulder City. (702) 294-3524. A 35-minute guided tour will take you through the dam and its power generating plant on the Colorado River. A visitor center at the top of the dam contains exhibits on its construction, operation, and history. Open year-round.

Oregon

The Hoover-Minthorn House. Newberg. (503) 538-6629. The boyhood home of Herbert Hoover is furnished with many items that belonged to Hoover's aunt and uncle, Laura and

John Minthorn. Hoover's bedroom contains his actual furniture. Open Wednesday–Sunday from March to November and weekends in December and February. Closed during January.

Virginia

Shenandoah National Park. Luray. (540) 999-3500. The buildings of Camp Rapidan have been preserved, and its name has been changed to Camp Hoover. Visits by car are limited; usually you must hike on park trails to reach the camp. On the weekend closest to Hoover's birthday (August 10), each year the National Park Service conducts camp tours by bus. Open year-round. Access may be restricted during winter months.

Washington, D.C.

The White House. (202) 456-7401. Several rooms are open to visitors on certain weekday mornings. You can get tickets when you arrive or in advance through your senator or congressperson. Open year-round.

Internet Addresses

Herbert Hoover Presidential Library
<http://hoover.nara.gov/welcome.html>

Herbert Hoover National Historic Site
<http://www.nps.gov/heho/>

Hoover Institution on War, Revolution, and Peace
<http://www.hoover.org/>

Index

A

American Relief Administration, 55

Anacostia Park, 9, 13

B

banks and banking, 74, 75–77, 79

Belgium, 48, 49–50, 51, 56, 71, 103

Bewick, Moreing & Company, 37, 38, 39, 43, 44, 45, 46

Black Tuesday, 75

Bonus Army, 9, *10*, 11, *12*, 13–14, 86–87

Boxer Rebellion, 40–43, 71

Boys Clubs of America, 101, 108, *109*

Boy Scouts, 72, 108

Branner, John, 28–29, 31

Brown, Mollie, 21

C

Camp Rapidan, 72, 88, 91

China, 19, 38–43, 51, 82, 96

Commission for Relief in Belgium (CRB), 50–51, 52, 55, 103

communism, 54–55, 58, 83

Congress, 8–9, 11, 60, 62, 71, 72–73, 78, 80, 83–84, *87*, 100

Coolidge, Calvin, 62, 63, 64, 108

D

Depression. *See* Great Depression.

E

economic conditions, 32, 34, 61, 63, 67, 71, 74, 79, 84–85

Eighteenth Amendment, 65

Eisenhower, Dwight D., 13, 100

F

farming and farmers, 53, 54, 71

Federal Aviation Agency (FAA), 110

Federal Communications Commission (FCC), 110

Food Administration, 52, 53, 54, 55

France, 38, 48, 51, 53, 55, 80, 97

Friends Service Committee, 56

G

Germany, 38, 48, 49, 50, 51, 52, 54, 56, 95, 96, 97

Girl Scouts, 72, 108

Gray, Jane, 25

Great Britain, 38, 48, 49, 53, 80, 81, 97

Great Depression, 8, 14, 77–78, 79–86, 95, 97, 103, 106–107, 112, 113

H

Harding, Warren, 61, 62

Harrison, Benjamin, 30

Hitler, Adolf, 96, 97

Hoover, Allan (son), 44, *46*, 64, 79, 94, 99, 105

Hoover, Allen (uncle), 21

Hoover, Benjah (uncle), 19

Hoover Commissions, 100, 111

Hoover Dam, 72, 95, 100, 110

Hoover, Herbert Jr. (son) , 44, *46*, 63–64, 94, 99, 105

Hoover, Hulda Minthorn (mother), 15–16, 17, 18, 19–21

Hoover Institution on War, Revolution, and Peace, 111

Hoover, Jesse (father), 15–16, 17, 18, 19

Hoover, Lou Henry (wife), 31–32, *33*, 34, 37, 38, 39, 40, 42, 43, 44, *46*, 49, 59, 69–70, 72, *83*, 88, 93, 98–99, 108, 110, 111

Hoover, Mary (sister), 18, 21, 23, 34, 35

Hoover, Theodore "Tad"(brother), 16, 19, 21, 23, 34, 35, 46, 50, 100–101
Hoover Tower, *6*, 111, *113*

J
Janin, Louis, 35
Japan, 38, 43, 81–82, 96, 98
Johnson, Lyndon B., 104

L
Landon, Alfred, 95
Latin America, 68–69, 111
London, England, 44, 46, 48–49, 107
London Naval Conference, 81

M
MacArthur, Douglas, 7, 11, 13–14
Mellon, Andrew, *83*, 86
Michelson, Charles, 88
Minthorn, John, 17, 22–23, 26, 28

N
national parks, 72
New Deal, 95, 97, 98, 100, 107, 111–112
New York City, 46, 65, 74, 98, 104, 107
New York Stock Exchange, 74, 75
Nixon, Richard, 104, 110

P
Pershing, John, 55–56
Prohibition, 65

Q
Quakers, 16, 17, 19, 20, 21, 22–23, 25, 31, 47, 56, 63, 66, 85, 91, 96, 107, 110

R
radio, 62–63, 66, 69, 74, 85, 88, 95, 97
Reconstruction Finance Corporation (RFC), 84

Roaring Twenties, 63, 74
Rogers, Will, 67, 84–85, 88, 90
Roosevelt, Franklin D., 14, 75, 87, 91, 92, 95, 96–97, 98, 99, 100, 107, 111
Roosevelt, Theodore, 68, 70
Russia, 38, 40, 43, 46, 48, 54, 85

S
San Francisco, California, 34, 35, 46, 107
Smith, Al, 65
Smoot-Hawley Tariff, 80–81
Stanford University, 25–26, 27–31, 32, 34, 37, 46, 47, 59, 63, 64, 93, 101, 110–111
Stimson Doctrine, 82
stock market crash, 73–74, 75–77
Swain, John, 26, 28

T
Tientsin, China, 38, 39, 40, *41*, *42*, 43
Truman, Harry S., 99, 100, *101*, 102, 105
Tugwell, Rexford, 111

U
unemployment, 32, 34, 61, 77, 78, 79, 81, 83, 84, 86, 93

W
Waldorf-Astoria, 98, 102
Warren, Earl, 104
West Branch, Iowa, 15, 19, 20, 103, 106
Willkie, Wendell L., 97
Wilson, Woodrow, 52, 54, 55, 101
World War I, 8, 48, 51–52, 53, 54, 61, 71, 80, 81, 82, 93, 96, 98, 99, 107, 111
World War II, 96, 98, 99, 100, 101, 107